English for Today's World

3

Joan Saslow ■ Allen Ascher

With *Top Notch Pop Songs and Karaoke*
by Rob Morsberger

Top Notch: English for Today's World 3

Pearson Education, 10 Bank Street, White Plains, NY 10606

Editorial director: Pamela Fishman
Senior development editor: Peter Benson
Vice president, director of design and production: Rhea Banker
Director of electronic production: Aliza Greenblatt
Managing editor: Mike Kemper
Production editor: Marc Oliver
Art director: Ann France
Senior manufacturing buyer: Dave Dickey
Photo research: Aerin Csigay
Digital layout specialist: Warren Fischbach
Text composition: Kirchoff-Wohlberg
Text font: Palatino 11/13
Cover photograph: "From Above," by Rhea Banker.
Copyright © 2005 Rhea Banker.

Library of Congress Cataloging-in-Publication Data

Saslow, Joan M.
Top notch : English for today's world. Student book. 2 / Joan Saslow, Allen Ascher.
p. cm.
1. English language—Textbooks for foreign speakers. 2. English language—Problems, exercises, etc. I. Ascher, Allen. II. Title.
PE1128.S2758 2006
428.2'4—dc22 2004048283

ISBN: 0-13-110634-1

Photo credits: All original photography by David Mager. Page 2 (Sydney) Peter Adams/Getty Images, (Cambridge) Steve Vidler/SuperStock, (London) Gail M. Shumway/Bruce Coleman, Inc., (Auckland) Rex A. Butcher/Bruce Coleman, Inc., (Edinburgh) Ken Sherman/Bruce Coleman, Inc., (San Francisco) Claver Carroll/PhotoLibrary.com, (Cape Town) Hein von Horsten/Gallo Images/Corbis, (New York) Jochen Tack/Peter Arnold, Inc., (Toronto) SuperStock; p. 5 (middle) Tom & Dee Ann McCarthy/Corbis; p. 7 (top) Russ Lappa, (bottom) Dave King/Dorling Kindersley; p. 9 Will & Deni McIntyre/Getty Images; p. 10 Elpida Memory, Inc.; p. 12 Royalty-Free/Corbis; p. 13 Angelo Cavalli/Getty Images; p. 14 (top) Dorling Kindersley, (left) Bob Daemmrich/The Image Works, (middle) Frozen Images/The Image Works, (right) Adam Woolfitt/Woodfin Camp & Associates; p. 17 Garry Gay/Mira.com; p. 19 (left to right) Will & Deni McIntyre/Photo Researchers, Inc., Maxine Hall/Corbis, Custom Medical Stock Photo, Inc., Lew Lause/SuperStock, Lester Lefkowitz/Corbis; p. 20 (top to bottom) Digital Vision Ltd./SuperStock, Sylvia Johnson/Woodfin Camp & Associates, Phil Schermeister/Corbis, Barbara P. Williams/Bruce Coleman Inc., Charles Gupton/Corbis, Paul Barton/Corbis; p. 22 (ragweed) Getty Images, (bacteria) David Spears/Corbis; p. 23 Royalty-Free/Corbis; p. 26 Arnulf Husmo/Getty Images; p. 29 Getty Images; p. 31 (left to right) Xerox Corporation, George Hall/Corbis, Michael Newman/PhotoEdit, Michelle D. Bridwell/PhotoEdit; p. 34 (caterer) Stewart Cohen/Getty Images, (DJ) Jeff Greenberg/The Image Works; p. 38 (top to bottom) V.O. Press/PhotoEdit, C Squared Studios/Getty Images, Olympus America Inc., Siede Preis/Getty Images, Siede Preis/Getty Images; p. 44 Benelux Press/Index Stock Imagery; p. 45 Steve Gorton/Dorling Kindersley; p. 46 (left) DPA/The Image Works, (right) Bettmann/Corbis; p. 47 (left) Steve Gorton/Dorling Kindersley, (right) Dorling Kindersley; p. 50 (background) Nancy R. Cohen/Getty Images, (top left) Russell Gordon/Odyssey, (top right) Hong Suk-young and Son Kwan-soo, (middle left) Steve Vidler/SuperStock, (middle right) Tony Freeman/PhotoEdit, (bottom left) Stephanie Maze/Woodfin Camp & Associates, (bottom right) AP Wide World Photos; p. 51 John Paul Endress; p. 52 (background) SuperStock, (cake) Michael Newman/PhotoEdit, (fireworks) SuperStock, (parades) Chip East/Corbis, (picnics) Michael Newman/PhotoEdit, (pray) Zafer Kizilkaya/Coral Planet, (gifts) Ryan McVay/Getty Images, (dead) Doug Martin/Photo Researchers, Inc., (costumes) Philip Gould/Corbis; p. 54 Steve Shott/Dorling Kindersley; p. 55 Stephen Hayward/Dorling Kindersley; p. 56 (top) Richard Powers/Corbis, (left) Mark Downey/Lucid Images, (right) Pablo Corral/Corbis; p. 57 Prentice Hall School Division; p. 58 (left) Elyse Lewin/Getty Images, (middle) Stockbyte/SuperStock, (right) Darama/Corbis; p. 62 (top left) Bettmann/Corbis, (top right) The Granger Collection, New York, (bottom) The Manila Times; p. 65 David Young-Wolff/PhotoEdit; p. 66 South Florida Sun-Sentinel. Reprinted with permission; p. 68 (all) Dorling Kindersley; p. 69 (all) Dorling Kindersley; p. 70 (top) Corbis, (bottom) Michael S. Yamashita/Corbis; p. 75 Henryk T. Kaiser/Index Stock Imagery; p. 79 (home) Ira Montgomery/Getty Images, (others) Dorling Kindersley; p. 80 (Spider-Man) Marvel; p. 86 (background) Philip Harvey/SuperStock, (wagon wheel) Carl & Ann Purcell/Corbis, (two-wheeled carts) Bettmann/Corbis, (horse-drawn) The Art Archive/Bibliotheque des Arts Decoratifs Paris/Dagli Orti, (potter's wheel) Blair Seitz/Photo Researchers, Inc., (auto) Ron Kimball/Ron Kimball Stock. All rights reserved; p. 87 (inset) Fadek Timothy/Corbis Sygma, (bottom) Science & Society Picture Library; p. 89 (camera) courtesy Canon USA, (monitor) IBM Corporation, (scanner) Michael Newman/PhotoEdit, (phone) SuperStock, (palmtop) Ryan McVay/Getty Images; p. 93 Dorling Kindersley; p. 94 (top left) North Wind Picture Archives, (top right) Science & Society Picture Library, (bottom) Inc., Martin Paul Ltd./Index Stock Imagery; p. 95 (left to right) Alinari/Art Resource, NY, Hulton Archive/Getty Images, Ray Ellis/Photo Researchers, Inc., Brown Brothers; p. 98 Reuters/Corbis; p. 104 NASA/Corbis; p. 111 Buddy Mays/Corbis; p. 113 (snake) Breck P. Kent/Animals Animals/Earth Scenes, (scorpion) Austin J. Stevens/Animals Animals/Earth Scenes, (shark) Brandon Cole/naturepl.com, (jellyfish) O.S.F./Animals Animals/Earth Scenes, (mosquito) Timothy Fadek/Corbis Sygma; p. 115 Robert Harding World Imagery/Getty Images; p. 116 (mountainous) Douglas Mason/Woodfin Camp & Associates, (hilly) David Weintraub/Photo Researchers, Inc., (flat) Jim Steinberg/Photo Researchers, Inc., (lush) K. H. Hanel/Panoramic Images/NGSImages.com, (arid) Jeff Foott/Bruce Coleman Inc., (forest) Jim Steinberg/Photo Researchers, Inc., (jungle) Gregory G. Dimijian/Photo Researchers, Inc., (canyon) T. Gervis/Robert Harding Picture Library, (island) Don Hebert/Getty Images, (valley) John Lamb/Getty Images; p. 117 (Galapagos) Alison Wright/Corbis, (Tahiti) N. DeVore III/Bruce Coleman, Inc., (Zambia) Hans Reinhard/Bruce Coleman, Inc., (Alaska) True North Images/www.agefotostock.com, (Tibet) Glen Allison/Getty Images, (bottom) Dorling Kindersley; p. 118 (background) Richard T. Nowitz/Corbis, (middle) Stephen Saks/Lonely Planet Images/Photo 20-20, (right top to bottom) SuperStock, Neil Duncan/PhotoLibrary.com, Mark Edwards/Peter Arnold, Inc., K. Ammann/Bruce Coleman Inc.; p. 119 (top) Dave G. Houser/Corbis, (middle) Ingo Arndt/naturepl.com (bottom).

Illustration credits: Steve Attoe, pp. 28, 92, 112; Kevin Brown / Top, p. 121; Sue Carlson, pp. 110, 114, 115, 120; Mark Collins, pp. 83, 92; Chris Gash, pp. 61, 97; Brian Hughes, pp. 27, 67; Stephen Hutchings, p. 82; Andy Myer, pp. 41, 102; Tom Newsom, pp. 25, 49, 73, 109; Dusan Petricic, pp. 17, 18, 24, 42, 43, 120; Gail Piazza, p. 16; Realia / Kirchoff Wohlberg, pp. 22, 26, 45, 46, 76; Robert Saunders, pp. 37, 85; Arvis Stewart, p. 86; Anne Veltfort, p. 35.

Printed in the United States of America
2 3 4 5 6 7 8 9 10–CRK–10 09 08 07 06 05

Contents

Scope and Sequence OF CONTENT AND SKILLS

UNIT	Vocabulary*	Social language	Grammar	GRAMMAR BOOSTER
1 **Cultural Literacy** *Page 2* *Top Notch* Song: "It's a Great Day for Love"	• Terms for describing manners, etiquette, and culture	• Make small talk with a stranger • Ask how someone would like to be addressed • Get to know someone	• Tag questions: form and social use • The past perfect: form and use	• Tag questions: more practice • Verb tense review: simple present, present continuous, present perfect and present perfect continuous, simple past and past continuous, used to, past perfect
2 **Health Matters** *Page 14*	• Dental emergencies • Symptoms • Medical procedures • Types of treatments and practitioners • Medications	• Make an appointment to see a dentist • Describe symptoms at a doctor's office • Show and acknowledge concern	• May, might, must, and be able to: possibility, conclusions, ability	• May, might, and must: degrees of certainty
3 **Getting Things Done** *Page 26* *Top Notch* Song: "I'll Get Back to You"	• Business and non-business services • Adjectives to describe services • Social events • Steps for planning a social event	• Request express service • Ask for a recommendation • Recommend and describe the qualities of a service provider	• The passive causative • Causatives get, have, and make	• The passive causative: the by phrase • Causatives get, have, and make: more practice • Let followed by an object and base form • Causative have and past perfect auxiliary have
4 **Life Choices** *Page 38*	• Fields for work or study • Reasons for changing your mind • Skills and abilities	• Greet someone you haven't seen for a while • Explain a change in life and work choices • Express regrets • Empathize	• Future in the past: was / were going to and would • Perfect modals: meaning and form	• Review: future with will and be going to • Review: future meaning with present continuous, simple present, and modals • Regrets about the past: wish + the past perfect; should have and ought to have
5 **Holidays and Traditions** *Page 50* *Top Notch* Song: "Endless Holiday"	• Types of holidays • Ways to commemorate a holiday • Wedding terminology	• Ask about and describe holiday traditions • Ask for advice about taboo and acceptable conversation topics • Explain holiday customs of your country	• Adjective clauses with subject relative pronouns • Adjective clauses with object relative pronouns	• Adjective clauses: more practice • Reciprocal pronouns: each other and one another • Reflexive pronouns • By + reflexive pronouns • Adjective clauses: who and whom for formal English

*In *Top Notch*, the term *vocabulary* refers to individual words, phrases, and expressions.

Speaking Activities	Pronunciation	Listening	Reading	Writing
• Make small talk with classmates • Identify rules of etiquette for visitors to your country • Discuss cultural changes	• Rising and falling intonation for tag questions	• Radio call-in show on etiquette Task: identify the topics discussed • People introducing themselves Task: determine how people prefer to be addressed	• Flyer for an international language school • Newspaper article about recent changes in Japanese culture • Survey about cultural changes	• Advise visitors about culture and etiquette in your country • Express your opinion on the importance of etiquette
• Role-play making a dentist appointment • Role-play a visit to a doctor's office • Discuss different types of medical treatments in your country • Compare types of medical treatments	• Intonation of lists	• Descriptions of dental emergencies Task: identify problems • Describing symptoms Task: check the symptoms described • Conversations between doctors and patients Task: complete patient information forms	• Health advice for international travelers • Overview of conventional and nontraditional health treatments	• Create a checklist for an international trip • Write about the kinds of health care you use • Complete patient information form
• Role-play requesting express service • Recommend a service provider • Plan a social event	• Emphatic stress to express enthusiasm	• Recommendations for service providers Task: identify the service required • Planning a social event Task: order the steps and note who will do each step • Requesting express service Task: describe customer needs	• Service provider's website • Tourist guide entry on buying custom-made clothing in Hong Kong	• Create an ad for a local service provider • Identify hard-to-find services • Write a story of a man's day, based on a complex illustration
• Describe changes in your life plans • Express regrets about life decisions • Interview a classmate about interests, qualifications, skills, and experience	• Reduction of have in perfect modals	• Conversations about changes in life plans Task: listen for the reasons the people changed their minds • Interviews at a job fair Task: match interviewees and qualifications • Conversations about regrets Task: infer whether there were regrets	• Work preference inventory • Skills inventory • Magazine article on the lifework of Mahatma Gandhi and Albert Schweitzer	• Recount the work and life decisions you have made and explain any regrets • Report on the life of a great humanitarian
• Role-play asking about and explaining local customs and traditions • Compare wedding proverbs from around the world • Describe wedding traditions to a visitor to your country	• Rhythm: "thought groups"	• Descriptions of holidays Task: identify the type of holiday and celebration • Lecture on traditional Indian wedding customs Task: correct the false statements • Conversations about weddings Task: determine each topic	• Magazine article describing three holiday traditions from around the world	• Describe in detail a holiday tradition in your country

Scope and Sequence OF CONTENT AND SKILLS

UNIT	Vocabulary	Social Language	Grammar	Grammar Booster
6 **Disasters and Emergencies** *Page 62* *Top Notch* Song: "Lucky to Be Alive"	• News sources • Severe weather events and other disasters • Emergency preparations and supplies • Terminology for discussing disasters	• Convey a message for a third person • Offer an excuse • Report news • Respond to good and bad news	• Indirect speech: imperatives • Indirect speech: say and tell; tense changes	• Punctuation rules for direct speech • Indirect speech: optional tense changes
7 **Books and Magazines** *Page 74*	• Types of books • Ways to describe reading material • Some ways to enjoy reading	• Recommend a book • Give and accept a compliment • Explain where you learned to make something • Offer to lend someone something	• Noun clauses: embedded questions • Noun clauses as direct objects	• Embedded questions: usage and punctuation • Embedded questions with infinitives • Noun clauses with that: after mental activity verbs • Noun clauses with that: after other expressions
8 **Inventions and Technology** *Page 86* *Top Notch* Song: "Reinvent the Wheel"	• Mechanical inventions in history • Ways to describe innovative products	• Describe a new product • Offer advice • Accept responsibility for a mistake • Reassure someone who has apologized	• Conditional sentences: review • The past unreal conditional	• Unless in conditional sentences • Clauses after wish • The unreal conditional: variety of forms
9 **Controversial Issues** *Page 98*	• Political terms and types of governments • Political and social beliefs • Controversial issues • Ways to disagree politely	• Ask if it's OK to discuss a topic • State your opinion • Express agreement • Disagree about controversial issues politely	• Non-count nouns for abstract ideas • Verbs followed by object and infinitive	• Count and non-count nouns • Gerunds and infinitives: form • Review: gerunds and infinitives after certain verbs
10 **Enjoying the World** *Page 110*	• Geographical features • Ways to describe possible risks • Dangerous animals and insects • Positive and negative descriptions • Ways to describe the natural world	• Warn about possible risks or dangers • Ask about and describe locations • Describe a natural setting • Recommend a place for its beauty	• Infinitives with too + adjective • Prepositions of place to describe locations	• Infinitives with too + adjective: more practice • Infinitives with enough • Prepositions usage • Proper nouns: capitalization • Proper nouns: use of the

Speaking Activities	Pronunciation	Listening	Reading	Writing
• Convey a message • Report what you heard on the news • Present plans for an emergency • Present "news reports" about historic disasters	• Direct and indirect speech: rhythm	• Weather reports Task: identify the weather event • Emergency radio broadcast Task: correct incorrect statements and report facts, using indirect speech • News report on natural disasters Task: identify the types of disasters	• Historic news headlines • Magazine article describing variables that affect an earthquake's severity	• Write about a historic disaster • Provide instructions on preparing for a disaster • Explain the factors that contribute to the severity of an earthquake
• Discuss what you've been reading • Explain where you learned something • Evaluate types of reading materials • Interview a classmate about reading habits	• Sentence stress in short answers with think, hope, guess, or believe	• Descriptions of reading habits Task: choose each speaker's preferences • Conversations about books Task: identify the type of book and infer if the speaker likes it	• Online bookstore website • Magazine article about the popularity of, and attitudes about, comic books	• Write about your reading habits • Review a book or other material you've read
• Discuss whether to purchase a product • Apologize for a mistake • Create and describe a "new invention" • Compare important inventions	• Contractions with 'd (would)	• People describing problems Task: select a useful invention for each person • Discussions of new products Task: determine which adjective best describes each product	• Magazine article describing the importance of the invention of the printing press	• Write about an invention that you think had a great impact
• Ask about acceptable discussion topics • Politely express an opinion about a controversial issue • Debate a controversial issue • Discuss global problems and suggest solutions	• Stress to emphasize meaning	• Conversations about politics and social beliefs Task: determine each person's political orientation • Opinions about controversial ideas Task: infer the speaker's opinion • People arguing their views Task: summarize arguments • Radio news program Task: identify the problems	• Authentic dictionary entries • Magazine article defining global problems	• Describe a local or world problem and offer possible solutions • Write the pros and cons of a controversial issue
• Warn someone to be careful • Recommend a tourist attraction • Describe a natural setting • Create a plan for economic development	• Voiced and voiceless th	• People discussing risks Task: infer if the place is safe • Description of a trip Task: identify natural features • Conversations about tourist destinations Task: infer if the speaker recommends going	• Authentic maps • Magazine article describing the pros and cons of eco-tourism	• Describe a spectacular natural setting • Plan eco-friendly development • Create a tourism advertisement

Acknowledgments

Top Notch International Advisory Board

The authors gratefully acknowledge the substantive and formative contributions of the members of the International Advisory Board.

CHERYL BELL, Middlesex County College, Middlesex, New Jersey, USA • **ELMA CABAHUG**, City College of San Francisco, San Francisco, California, USA • **JO CARAGATA**, Mukogawa Women's University, Hyogo, Japan • **ANN CARTIER**, Palo Alto Adult School, Palo Alto, California, USA • **TERRENCE FELLNER**, Himeji Dokkyo University, Hyogo, Japan • **JOHN FUJIMORI**, Meiji Gakuin High School, Tokyo, Japan • **ARETA ULHANA GALAT**, Escola Superior de Estudos Empresariais e Informática, Curitiba, Brazil • **DOREEN M. GAYLORD**, Kanazawa Technical College, Ishikawa, Japan • **EMILY GEHRMAN**, Newton International College, Garden Grove, California, USA • **ANN-MARIE HADZIMA**, National Taiwan University, Taipei, Taiwan • **KAREN KYONG-AI PARK**, Seoul National University, Seoul, Korea • **ANA PATRICIA MARTÍNEZ VITE DIP. R.S.A.**, Universidad del Valle de México, Mexico City, Mexico • **MICHELLE ANN MERRITT, PROULEX/** Universidad de Guadalajara, Guadalajara, Mexico • **ADRIANNE P. OCHOA**, Georgia State University, Atlanta, Georgia, USA • **LOUIS PARDILLO**, Korea Herald English Institute, Seoul, Korea • **THELMA PERES**, Casa Thomas Jefferson, Brasilia, Brazil • **DIANNE RUGGIERO**, Broward Community College, Davie, Florida, USA • **KEN SCHMIDT**, Tohoku Fukushi University, Sendai, Japan • **ALISA A. TAKEUCHI**, Garden Grove Adult Education, Garden Grove, California, USA • **JOSEPHINE TAYLOR**, Centro Colombo Americano, Bogotá, Colombia • **PATRICIA VECIÑO**, Instituto Cultural Argentino Norteamericano, Buenos Aires, Argentina • **FRANCES WESTBROOK**, AUA Language Center, Bangkok, Thailand

Reviewers and Piloters

Many thanks also to the reviewers and piloters all over the world who reviewed *Top Notch* in its final form.

G. Julian Abaqueta, Huachiew Chalermprakiet University, Samutprakarn, Thailand • **David Aline**, Kanagawa University, Kanagawa, Japan • **Marcia Alves**, Centro Cultural Brasil Estados Unidos, Franca, Brazil • **Yousef Al-Yacoub**, Qatar Petroleum, Doha, Qatar • **Maristela Barbosa Silveira e Silva**, Instituto Cultural Brasil-Estados Unidos, Manaus, Brazil • **Beth Bartlett**, Centro Colombo Americano, Cali, Colombia • **Carla Battigelli**, University of Zulia, Maracaibo, Venezuela • **Claudia Bautista**, C.B.C., Caracas, Venezuela • **Rob Bell**, Shumei Yachiyo High School, Chiba, Japan • **Dr. Maher Ben Moussa**, Sharjah University, Sharjah, United Arab Emirates • **Elaine Cantor**, Englewood Senior High School, Jacksonville, Florida, USA • **María Aparecida Capellari**, **SENAC**, São Paulo, Brazil • **Eunice Carrillo Ramos**, Colegio Durango, Naucalpan, Mexico • **Janette Carvalhinho de Oliveira**, Centro de Linguas (UFES), Vitória, Brazil • **María Amelia Carvalho Fonseca**, Centro Cultural Brasil-Estados Unidos, Belém, Brazil • **Audy Castañeda**, Instituto Pedagógico de Caracas, Caracas, Venezuela • **Ching-Fen Chang**, National Chiao Tung University, Hsinchu, Taiwan • **Ying-Yu Chen**, Chinese Culture University, Taipei, Taiwan • **Joyce Chin**, The Language Training and Testing Center, Taipei, Taiwan • **Eun Cho**, Pagoda Language School, Seoul, Korea • **Hyungzung Cho**, MBC Language Institute, Seoul, Korea • **Dong Sua Choi**, MBC Language Institute, Seoul, Korea • **Jeong Mi Choi**, Freelancer, Seoul, Korea • **Peter Chun**, Pagoda Language School, Seoul, Korea • **Eduardo Corbo**, Legacy ELT, Salto, Uruguay • **Marie Cosgrove**, Surugadai University, Saitama, Japan • **María Antonieta Covarrubias Souza**, Centro Escolar Akela, Mexico City, Mexico • **Katy Cox**, Casa Thomas Jefferson, Brasilia, Brazil • **Michael Donovan**, Gakushuin University, Tokyo, Japan • **Stewart Dorward**, Shumei Eiko High School, Saitama, Japan • **Ney Eric Espina**, Centro Venezolano Americano del Zulia, Maracaibo, Venezuela • **Edith Espino**, Centro Especializado de Lenguas - Universidad Tecnológica de Panamá, El Dorado, Panama • **Allen P. Fermon**, Instituto Brasil-Estados Unidos, Ceará, Brazil • **Simão Ferreira Banha**, Phil Young's English School, Curitiba, Brazil • **María Elena Flores Lara**, Colegio Mercedes, Mexico City, Mexico • **Valesca Fróis Nassif**, Associação Cultural Brasil-Estados Unidos, Salvador, Brazil • **José Fuentes**, Empire Language Consulting, Caracas, Venezuela • **José Luis Guerrero**, Colegio Cristóbal Colón, Mexico City, Mexico • **Claudia Patricia Gutiérrez**, Centro Colombo Americano, Cali, Colombia • **Valerie Hansford**, Asia University, Tokyo, Japan • **Gene Hardstark**, Dotkyo University, Saitama, Japan • **Maiko Hata**, Kansai University, Osaka, Japan • **Susan Elizabeth Haydock Miranda de Araujo**, Centro Cultural Brasil Estados Unidos, Belém, Brazil • **Gabriela Herrera**, Fundametal, Valencia, Venezuela • **Sandy Ho**, GEOS International, New York, New York, USA • **Yuri Hosoda**, Showa Women's University, Tokyo, Japan • **Hsiao-I Hou**, Shu-Te University, Kaohsiung County, Taiwan • **Kuei-ping Hsu**, National Tsing Hua University, Hsinchu, Taiwan • **Chia-yu Huang**, National Tsing Hua University, Hsinchu, Taiwan • **Caroline C. Hwang**, National Taipei University of Science and Technology, Taipei, Taiwan • **Diana Jones**, Angloamericano, Mexico City, Mexico • **Eunjeong Kim**, Freelancer, Seoul, Korea • **Julian Charles King**, Qatar Petroleum, Doha, Qatar • **Bruce Lee**, CIE: Foreign Language Institute, Seoul, Korea • **Myunghee Lee**, MBC Language Institute, Seoul, Korea • **Naidnapa Leoprasertkul**, Language Development Center, Mahasarakham University, Mahasarakham, Thailand • **Eleanor S. Leu**, Souchow University, Taipei, Taiwan • **Eliza Liu**, Chinese Culture University, Taipei, Taiwan • **Carlos Lizárraga**, Angloamericano, Mexico City, Mexico • **Philippe Loussarevian**, Keio University Shonan Fujisawa High School, Kanagawa, Japan • **Jonathan Lynch**, Azabu University, Tokyo, Japan • **Thomas Mach**, Konan University, Hyogo, Japan • **Lilian Mandel Civatti**, Associação Cultural Brasil-Estados Unidos, Salvador, Brazil • **Hakan Mansuroglu**, Zoni Language Center, West New York, New Jersey, USA • **Martha McGaughey**, Language Training Institute, Englewood Cliffs, New Jersey, USA • **David Mendoza Plascencia**, Instituto Internacional de Idiomas, Naucalpan, Mexico • **Theresa Mezo**, Interamerican University, Río Piedras, Puerto Rico • **Luz Adriana Montenegro Silva**, Colegio CAFAM, Bogotá, Colombia • **Magali de Moraes Menti**, Instituto Lingua, Porto Alegre, Brazil • **Massoud Moslehpour**, The Overseas Chinese Institute of Technology, Taichung, Taiwan • **Jennifer Nam**, IKE, Seoul, Korea • **Marcos Norelle F. Victor**, Instituto Brasil-Estados Unidos, Ceará, Brazil • **Luz María Olvera**, Instituto Juventud del Estado de México, Naucalpan, Mexico • **Roxana Orrego Ramírez**, Universidad Diego Portales, Santiago, Chile • **Ming-Jong Pan**, National Central University, Jhongli City, Taiwan • **Sandy Park**, Topia Language School, Seoul, Korea • **Patrícia Elizabeth Peres Martins**, Instituto Brasil-Estados Unidos, Rio de Janeiro, Brazil • **Rodrigo Peza**, Passport Language Centers, Bogotá, Colombia • **William Porter**, Osaka Institute of Technology, Osaka, Japan • **Caleb Prichard**, Kwansei Gakuin University, Hyogo, Japan • **Mirna Quintero**, Instituto Pedagógico de Caracas, Caracas, Venezuela • **Roberto Rabbini**, Seigakuin University, Saitama, Japan • **Terri Rapoport**, Berkeley College, White Plains, New York, USA • **Yvette Rieser**, Centro Electrónico de Idiomas, Maracaibo, Venezuela • **Orlando Rodríguez**, New English Teaching School, Paysandu, Uruguay • **Mayra Rosario**, Pontificia Universidad Católica Madre y Maestra, Santiago, Dominican Republic • **Peter Scout**, Sakura no Seibo Junior College, Fukushima, Japan • **Jungyeon Shim**, EG School, Seoul, Korea • **Keum Ok Song**, MBC Language Institute, Seoul, Korea • **Assistant Professor Dr. Reongrudee Soonthornmanee**, Chulalongkorn University Language Institute, Bangkok, Thailand • **Claudia Stanisclause**, The Language College, Maracay, Venezuela • **Tom Suh**, The Princeton Review, Seoul, Korea • **Phiphawin Suphawat**, KhonKaen University, KhonKaen, Thailand • **Craig Sweet**, Poole Gakuin Junior and Senior High Schools, Osaka, Japan • **Yi-nien Josephine Twu**, National Tsing Hua University, Hsinchu, Taiwan • **Maria Christina Uchôa Close**, Instituto Cultural Brasil-Estados Unidos, São José dos Campos, Brazil • **Luz Vanegas Lopera**, Lexicom The Place For Learning English, Medellín, Colombia • **Julieta Vasconcelos García**, Centro Escolar del Lago, A.C., Mexico City, Mexico • **Carol Vaughan**, Kanto Kokusai High School, Tokyo, Japan • **Patricia Celia Veciño**, Instituto Cultural Argentino Norteamericano, Buenos Aires, Argentina • **Isabela Villas Boas**, Casa Thomas Jefferson, Brasilia, Brazil • **Iole Vitti**, Peanuts English School, Poços de Caldas, Brazil • **Gabi Witthaus**, Qatar Petroleum, Doha, Qatar • **Yi-Ling Wu**, Shih Chien University, Taipei, Taiwan • **Chad Wynne**, Osaka Keizai University, Osaka, Japan • **Belkis Yanes**, Freelance Instructor, Caracas, Venezuela • **I-Chieh Yang**, Chung-kuo Institute of Technology, Taipei, Taiwan • **Emil Ysona**, Instituto Cultural Dominico-Americano, Santo Domingo, Dominican Republic • **Chi-fang Yu**, Soo Chow University, Taipei, Taiwan, • **Shigeki Yusa**, Sendai Shirayuri Women's College, Sendai, Japan

To the Teacher

What is *Top Notch*?

- *Top Notch* is a six-level communicative English course for adults and young adults, with two beginning entry levels.
- *Top Notch* prepares students to interact successfully and confidently with both native and non-native speakers of English.
- *Top Notch* demonstrably brings students to a "Top Notch" level of communicative competence.

Key Elements of the *Top Notch* Instructional Design

Concise two-page lessons

Each easy-to-teach two-page lesson is designed for one class session and begins with a clearly stated communication goal and ends with controlled or free communication practice. Each lesson provides vocabulary, grammar, and social language contextualized in all four skills, keeping the pace of a class session lively and varied.

Daily confirmation of progress

Adult and young adult students need to observe and confirm their own progress. In *Top Notch*, students conclude each class session with a controlled or free practice activity that demonstrates their ability to use new vocabulary, grammar, and social language. This motivates and keeps students eager to continue their study of English and builds their pride in being able to speak accurately, fluently, and authentically.

Real language

Carefully exposing students to authentic, natural English, both receptively and productively, is a necessary component of building understanding and expression. All conversation models feature the language people really use; nowhere to be found is "textbook English" written merely to exemplify grammar.

Practical content

In addition to classic topical vocabulary, grammar, and conversation, *Top Notch* includes systematic practice of highly practical language, such as: how to describe symptoms at a doctor's office, and how to ask for express service at a service provider such as a dry cleaner or copy center. In addition to these practical applications, *Top Notch* continues development of its discussion syllabus with popular discussion topics ranging from explaining the holiday customs of one's country to polite discussions of government and politics—usable language today's students want and need.

Memorable model conversations

Effective language instruction must make language memorable. The full range of social and functional communicative needs is presented through practical model conversations that are intensively practiced and manipulated, first within a guided model and then in freer and more personalized formats.

High-impact vocabulary syllabus

In order to ensure students' solid acquisition of vocabulary essential for communication, *Top Notch* contains explicit presentation, practice, and systematic extended recycling of words, collocations, and expressions appropriate at each level of study. The extensive captioned illustrations, photos, definitions, examples, and contextualized sentences remove doubts about meaning and provide a permanent in-book reference for student test preparation. An added benefit is that teachers don't have to search for pictures to bring to class and don't have to resort to translating vocabulary into the students' native language.

Learner-supportive grammar

Grammar is approached explicitly and cognitively, through form, meaning, and use—both within the Student's Book units and in a bound-in Grammar Booster. Charts provide examples and paradigms enhanced by simple usage notes at students' level of comprehension. This takes the guesswork out of meaning, makes lesson preparation easier for teachers, and provides students with comprehensible charts for permanent reference and test preparation. All presentations of grammar are followed by exercises to ensure adequate practice.

English as an international language

Top Notch prepares students for interaction with both native and non-native speakers of English, both linguistically and culturally. English is treated as an international language, rather than the language of a particular country or region. In addition, *Top Notch* helps students develop a cultural fluency by creating an awareness of the varied rules across cultures for: politeness, greetings and introductions, appropriateness of dress in different settings, conversation do's and taboos, table manners, and other similar issues.

Two beginning-level texts

Beginning students can be placed either in *Top Notch 1* or *Top Notch Fundamentals*, depending on ability and background. Even absolute beginners can start with confidence in *Top Notch Fundamentals*. False beginners can begin with *Top Notch 1*. The *Top Notch Placement Test* clarifies the best placement within the series.

Estimated teaching time

Each level of *Top Notch* is designed for 60 to 90 instructional hours and contains a full range of supplementary components and enrichment devices to tailor the course to individual needs.

Components of *Top Notch 3*

Student's Book

The Student's Book contains a bound-in Grammar Booster and Student's Take-Home Audio CD with pronunciation/intonation practice and the *Top Notch Pop* songs.

Teacher's Edition and Lesson Planner

Complete yet concise lesson plans are provided for each class. Corpus notes provide essential information from the *Longman Spoken American Corpus* and the *Longman Learner's Corpus*. In addition, a free *Teacher's Resource Disk* offers the following printable extension activities to personalize your teaching style:

- Grammar self-checks
- *Top Notch Pop* song activities
- Writing process worksheets
- Learning strategies
- Pronunciation activities and supplements
- Extra reading comprehension activities
- Vocabulary cards and cumulative vocabulary activities
- Graphic organizers
- Pair work cards

Copy & Go: Ready-made Interactive Activities for Busy Teachers

Interactive games, puzzles, and other practice activities in convenient photocopiable form support the Student's Book content and provide a welcome change of pace.

Complete Classroom Audio Program

The audio program, available in cassette or audio CD format, contains listening comprehension activities, rhythm and intonation practice, and targeted pronunciation activities that focus on accurate and comprehensible pronunciation.

Because *Top Notch* prepares students for international communication, a variety of native *and* non-native speakers are included to ready students for the world outside the classroom. The audio program also includes the five *Top Notch Pop* songs in standard and karaoke form.

Workbook

A tightly linked illustrated Workbook contains exercises that provide additional practice and reinforcement of language concepts and skills from *Top Notch* and its Grammar Booster.

Complete Assessment Package with *ExamView®* Software

Ten easy-to-administer and easy-to-score unit achievement tests assess listening, vocabulary, grammar, social language, reading, and writing. Two review tests, one mid-book and one end-of-book, provide additional cumulative assessment. Two speaking tests assess progress in speaking. In addition to the photocopiable achievement tests, *ExamView®* software enables teachers to tailor-make tests to best meet their needs by combining items in any way they wish.

Top Notch TV

A lively and entertaining video offers a TV-style situation comedy that reintroduces language from each *Top Notch* unit, plus authentic unrehearsed interviews with English speakers from around the world and authentic karaoke. Packaged with the video are activity worksheets and a booklet with teaching suggestions and complete video scripts.

Companion Website

A Companion Website at www.longman.com/topnotch provides numerous additional resources for students and teachers. This no-cost, high-benefit feature includes opportunities for further practice of language and content from the *Top Notch* Student's Book.

Welcome to Top Notch!

About the Authors

Joan Saslow

Joan Saslow has taught English as a Foreign Language and English as a Second Language to adults and young adults in both South America and the United States. She taught English and French at the Binational Centers of Valparaíso and Viña del Mar, Chile, and the Catholic University of Valparaíso. In the United States, Ms. Saslow taught English as a Foreign Language to Japanese university students at Marymount College and to international students in Westchester Community College's intensive English program as well as workplace English at the General Motors auto assembly plant in Tarrytown, NY.

Ms. Saslow is the series director of Longman's popular five-level adult series ***True Colors: An EFL Course for Real Communication*** and of ***True Voices***, a five-level video course. She is author of ***Ready to Go: Language, Lifeskills, and Civics***, a four-level adult ESL series; ***Workplace Plus***, a vocational English series; and of ***Literacy Plus***, a two-level series that teaches literacy, English, and culture to adult pre-literate students. She is also author of ***English in Context: Reading Comprehension for Science and Technology***, a three-level series for English for special purposes. In addition, Ms. Saslow has been an author, an editor of language teaching materials, a teacher-trainer, and a frequent speaker at gatherings of EFL and ESL teachers for over thirty years.

Allen Ascher

Allen Ascher has been a teacher and teacher-trainer in both China and the United States, as well as an administrator and a publisher. Mr. Ascher specialized in teaching listening and speaking to students at the Beijing Second Foreign Language Institute, to hotel workers at a major international hotel in China, and to Japanese students from Chubu University studying English at Ohio University. In New York, Mr. Ascher taught students of all language backgrounds and abilities at the City University of New York, and he trained teachers in the TESOL Certificate Program at the New School. He was also the academic director of the International English Language Institute at Hunter College.

Mr. Ascher has provided lively workshops for EFL teachers throughout Asia, Latin America, Europe, and the Middle East. He is author of the popular ***Think about Editing: A Grammar Editing Guide for ESL Writers***. As a publisher, Mr. Ascher played a key role in the creation of some of the most widely used materials for adults, including: ***True Colors, NorthStar, Focus on Grammar, Global Links***, and ***Ready to Go***. Mr. Ascher has an M.A. in Applied Linguistics from Ohio University.

UNIT 1

Cultural Literacy

UNIT GOALS

1 Meet someone and make small talk
2 Get to know someone
3 Be culturally literate
4 Discuss how culture changes over time

TOPIC PREVIEW. Look at the flyer for an international language school. Choose a place to study English.

Study Abroad Opportunities
EnglishSOURCE
YOUR TICKET TO THE WORLD OF ENGLISH
Choose from one of our 9 international sites
Sydney
Harbor city with a cultural flair
Auckland
With a background rhythm of Polynesian culture
Cape Town
Pristine beaches and a cultural melting pot

Shop and compare. EnglishSOURCE offers:

- an international student body—over 35 countries represented!
- courses tailored to your available time—from one week to one year
- native teachers with university degrees
- arranged homestays near classes
- guaranteed achievement—or your money back!

Historic city—world-renowned university—community of scholars

Magnificent—from the medieval to the modern

Capital of the world

The birthplace of English—home of the Crown

Human-size city—a delight for the eyes—near ocean and mountain peaks

Canada's largest city—never run out of things to do, see, or buy

PAIR WORK. Which site did you choose? Why?

- ☐ because of the location
- ☐ because of the type of English spoken there
- ☐ because I have friends or relatives there
- ☐ other reason(s): ____________________

C SOUND BITES. Read along silently as you listen to a conversation at a business meeting in Thailand.

TERESA: Allow me to introduce myself. I'm Teresa Segovia, from Santiago, Chile. *Sawatdee-Kaa.*
SURAT: Where did you learn the *wai*?*
TERESA: Actually, a Thai friend in Chile taught me.

SURAT: *Sawatdee-Khrab.* Nice to meet you, Ms. Segovia. I'm Surat Leekpai.
TERESA: Nice to meet you, too. But please call me Terri.
SURAT: And please call me Surat. It's easier to say than Leekpai!

*Thais greet each other with a gesture called the "wai" and by saying "Sawatdee-Kaa" (women) / "Sawatdee-Khrab (men)."

TERESA: Do you mind my asking you the custom here? Are most people on a first-name basis?
SURAT: At company meetings in English, absolutely. In general, though, it's probably best to watch what others do. You know what they say: "When in Rome..."
TERESA: M-hmm... "do as the Romans do!"

D DISCUSSION.

1. Why do you think Teresa greets Surat with the *wai*?
2. Why do Surat and Teresa say, "When in Rome, do as the Romans do!"?
3. When do you think people should use first names with each other? When do you think they should use titles and last names?

WHAT ABOUT **YOU?**

If you take a trip to another country, how would you like to be addressed?

☐ 1. I'd like to be called by my title and my family name.
☐ 2. I'd like to be called by my first name.
☐ 3. I'd like to be called by my nickname.
☐ 4. I'd prefer to follow the local customs.

LESSON 1

Meet Someone and Make Small Talk

CONVERSATION MODEL Read and listen.

A: Good morning. Beautiful day, isn't it?
B: It really is. By the way, I'm Kazuko Toshinaga.
A: I'm Jane Quitt. Nice to meet you.
B: Nice to meet you, too.
A: Do you mind if I call you Kazuko?
B: Absolutely not. Please do.
A: And please call me Jane.

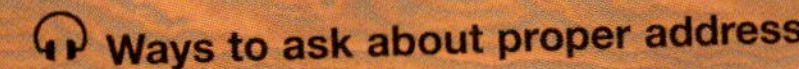

Ways to ask about proper address

Do you mind if I call you [Kazuko]?
Would it be rude to call you [Kazuko]?
What would you like to be called?
How do you prefer to be addressed?
Do you use Ms. or Mrs.?

Rhythm and intonation practice

GRAMMAR. Tag questions: form and social use

Use tag questions to confirm information you already think is true or to encourage someone to make small talk.

statement	tag question	answer
You're Kazuko,	**aren't you**?	Yes, I am. / No, I'm not.
You speak Thai,	**don't you**?	Yes, I do. / No, I don't.
They'll be here later,	**won't they**?	Yes, they will. / No, they won't.
They didn't know,	**did they**?	Yes, they did. / No, they didn't.
It's a beautiful day,	**isn't it**?	Yes, it is. / No, it isn't.

When the statement is affirmative, the tag question is negative. When the statement is negative, the tag question is affirmative.

He**'s** late, **isn't** he? He **isn't** late, **is** he?

BE CAREFUL! Use pronouns, not names or nouns, in tag questions.

Machu Picchu was built by the Incas, wasn't it? (NOT ~~wasn't Machu Picchu?~~)

Use aren't for negative tag questions after I am.

I'm on time, **aren't** I? BUT I'm not late, am I?

GRAMMAR BOOSTER

PAGE G1
For more …

PRONUNCIATION. Intonation of tag questions. Read and listen. Then listen again and repeat.

Use rising intonation when you're not sure if the listener will agree, and you expect an answer.

People use first names here, don't they?

That movie was great, wasn't it?

Use falling intonation when you think the listener will agree.

It's a beautiful day for a walk, isn't it?

You're studying in Chicago next year, aren't you?

C **Complete each statement with a tag question.**

1. Robert Reston is the director of the English program, ________?
2. There weren't any openings at the San Francisco location, ________?
3. They're all going to enroll in the Chicago course, ________?
4. I'm not too late to sign up, ________?
5. She prefers to be addressed by her title and last name, ________?
6. The letters of acceptance will be mailed in March, ________?
7. Australia has been a terrific place to learn English, ________?
8. It was a great day, ________?

PAIR WORK. Write a few facts about yourself. Give the paper to your partner to read for a minute. Then take back the paper and confirm the information with tag questions.

I grew up here, but my parents are from Italy. I started studying English when I was in primary school.

"Your parents are from Italy, aren't they?"

CONVERSATION PAIR WORK

Meet your classmates. Ask them how they'd like to be addressed. Use tag questions to make small talk about the weather and other subjects.

LESSON 2

Get to Know Someone

CONVERSATION MODEL Read and listen.

A: Hi. I'm Sylvia Contreras.
B: Conrad Schmitt. Nice to meet you, Sylvia. You know, you look familiar. You were in this class last term, weren't you?
A: No, actually, I wasn't. I hadn't arrived here yet when the class began.

Rhythm and intonation practice

A GRAMMAR. The past perfect: form and use

Form the past perfect with <u>had</u> and a past participle of the main verb.

past participle
By 2001, she **had** already **met** her husband.

Use the past perfect to describe something that happened before a specific time in the past.

By April, he **had started** his new job.
At 3:00, we **hadn't** yet **heard** the news.

Use the past perfect with the simple past tense to show which of two past events occurred first.

I **had** already **seen** the movie when it **came** out on DVD. (First I saw it. Then it came out on DVD.)

Note that in informal speech we often use the simple past tense instead of the past perfect. The words <u>before</u> and <u>after</u> can help clarify the order of the events in informal speech.

By April, he started his new job.
Before I graduated, I learned to speak Greek.
I became a good driver after I got my own car.

PAGES G1–G3
For more ...

B Choose the correct meaning for each statement.

1. "When they decided to open a language school in Scotland, I had already decided to study in San Francisco."
   - ☐ First they decided to open the language school in Scotland. Then I decided to study in San Francisco.
   - ☐ First I decided to study in San Francisco. Then they opened a language school in Scotland.
2. "By the time she was twenty, she had studied at two language schools."
   - ☐ She turned twenty before she studied at two language schools.
   - ☐ First she studied at two language schools. Then she turned twenty.
3. "We had already applied for the study abroad program when they canceled it."
   - ☐ First we applied for the program. Then they canceled it.
   - ☐ First they canceled the program. Then we applied for it.

4. "I had received my acceptance letter when they closed the school."
☐ First I received my acceptance letter. Then they closed the school.
☐ First they closed the school. Then I received my acceptance letter.

C **Lynn Todd is taking a weekend trip. It's almost 6:00 P.M. Read her "to-do" list and complete the statements, using <u>already</u> or <u>not yet</u>.**

1. At 8:30 Lynn had already dropped off her jacket, but she hadn't yet taken the cats to Mara's house.
2. By 11:00 she ________________ the cats to Mara's house, but she ________________ for the weekend.
3. At 12:45 she ________________ lunch with Lainie, but she ________________ the car.
4. By 2:10 she ________________ the books to the library, but she ________________ her exam.
5. At 5:15 she ________________ Paul, but she ________________ her jacket at the dry cleaners.

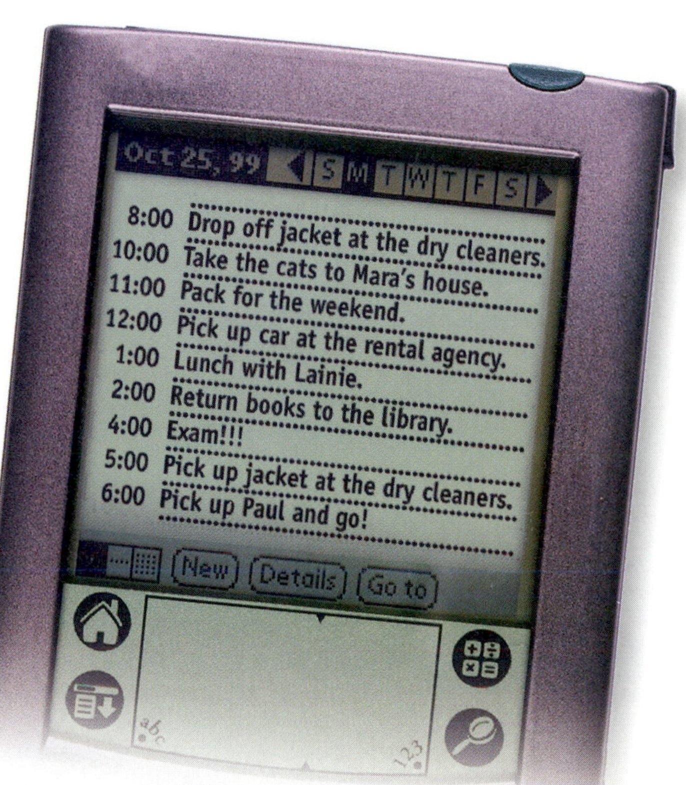

12:00 Pick up car at the rental agency.

6:00 Pick up Paul and go!

CONVERSATION PAIR WORK

Role-play getting to know someone, using one of the imaginary situations. Use the guide, or create a new conversation.

A: _____, I'm _____.
B: _____. Nice to meet you, _____. You know, you look familiar. _____?
A: _____...

Continue the conversation in your <u>own</u> way.

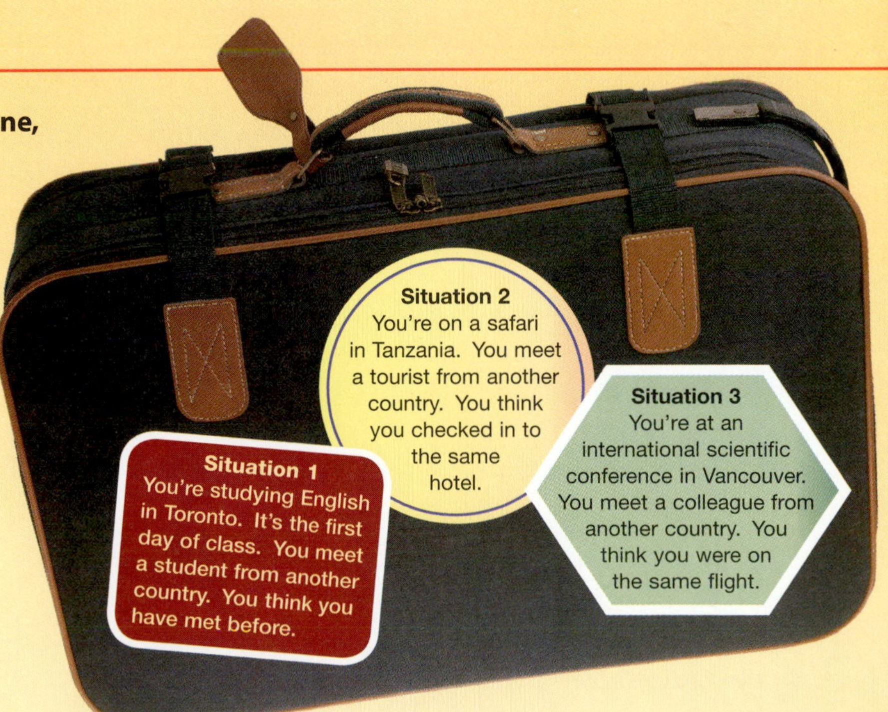

Situation 1
You're studying English in Toronto. It's the first day of class. You meet a student from another country. You think you have met before.
Situation 2
You're on a safari in Tanzania. You meet a tourist from another country. You think you checked in to the same hotel.
Situation 3
You're at an international scientific conference in Vancouver. You meet a colleague from another country. You think you were on the same flight.

LESSON

3 Be Culturally Literate

A VOCABULARY. Manners and etiquette. Listen and practice.

etiquette the "rules" of polite behavior

When traveling, it's important to be aware of the etiquette of the culture you will be visiting.

cultural literacy knowing about and respecting the culture of others and following their rules of etiquette when interacting with them

In today's world, cultural literacy is essential to success and good relations with others.

table manners rules for polite behavior when eating with other people

Table manners differ from culture to culture.

punctuality the social "rules" about being on time

Punctuality is considered more important in some cultures than in others.

impolite not polite, rude

All cultures have rules for polite and impolite behavior.

offensive extremely rude or impolite

In some cultures, it's offensive to take pictures of people without their permission.

customary usual or traditional in a particular culture

In many cultures, handshakes are customary when meeting someone for the first time.

taboo not allowed because of very strong cultural or religious rules against behavior or topics that are considered very offensive

It's taboo to eat pork in some religions.

B DISCUSSION.

1. What are some good ways to teach children etiquette? Give specific examples, using words from the vocabulary.
2. Do you know any differences between your culture and others?
3. Why do you think table manners are important in almost all cultures?

C LISTENING COMPREHENSION. Listen to three calls from a radio show. Then look at the chart and listen again to each call. Check the subjects that were discussed.

What subjects were discussed?	1. Arturo and Jettrin	2. Hiroko and Nadia	3. Javier and Sujeet
table manners	☐	☐	☐
greetings	☐	☐	☐
dress and clothing	☐	☐	☐
male and female behavior	☐	☐	☐
taboos	☐	☐	☐
offensive behavior	☐	☐	☐
punctuality	☐	☐	☐
language	☐	☐	☐

D DISCUSSION. In small groups, summarize the information from each of the calls on the radio show. Listen again if necessary.

TOP NOTCH
INTERACTION • *Know before you go!*

STEP 1. PAIR WORK. On the notepad, make notes about what visitors to your country should know.

STEP 2. DISCUSSION. Combine everyone's notes on the board. Does everyone agree?

STEP 3. WRITING. Write an article to help a visitor be culturally literate about your country. Use important information from your notepad and the board.

How do people greet each other when they meet for the first time?

Are greetings customs different for men and women? How?

When and how do you address people formally?

When and how do you address people informally?

What are some do's and don'ts for table manners?

Are certain foods or beverages taboo?

What are some taboo conversation topics?

What are the customs about punctuality?

What is a customary gift if you are visiting someone's home?

Are there any gift taboos (kinds of flowers, etc.)?

Are there some situations or places where you should dress modestly?

What else should a visitor know?

Discuss How Culture Changes over Time

LESSON

READING WARM-UP. Can you think of an example of how etiquette and culture change over time?

READING. Read the article. Is Japanese culture more or less formal than it was in the past?

Japanese Workers Get Word from on High: Drop Formality

By NORIMITSU ONISHI

HIROSHIMA, Japan, Oct. 30, 2003 — The change in policy came directly from the Tokyo headquarters of Elpida Memory, a semiconductor maker.

Elpida's 1,366 workers were told to stop addressing each other by their titles and simply to add the suffix -san to their names. Many Japanese have dropped the use of titles to create a more open — and, they hope, competitive — culture. This change mirrors other changes in Japanese society, experts say. Equality-minded parents no longer emphasize honorific language to their children, and most schools no longer expect children to use honorific language to their teachers. What is clear is that the use of honorific language, called keigo, to elevate a person or humble oneself, has especially fallen out of use among young Japanese.

Naomi Sugi, a secretary at the Elpida factory, has hesitantly begun addressing her boss as "Mr. Yamamoto" instead of "President Yamamoto."

Japanese, perhaps more than any other language, has long taken account of social standing. In Japanese, there are many ways to say I or you, calibrated by age, circumstance, gender, social position and other factors. Verb endings, adjectives and entire words also shift according to the situation.

These days, companies hope the use of -san — less cumbersome than the longer titles traditionally used — will allow workers to exchange ideas more freely and make decisions more quickly. In 2001, 59 percent of companies with more than 3,000 employees had adopted such a policy, compared with 34 percent in 1995, according to the Institute of Labor Administration of Japan.

"It's easier to talk now," said Kazuyoshi Iizuka, a 32-year-old employee at the Tokyo headquarters of Elpida. The factory's president, Takehiko Kubota, 59, who describes himself as "old-fashioned," sent an e-mail message on Sept. 5 explaining the policy to his staff.

Answer the following questions, according to the information in the article.

1. What are some recent changes in the social use of the Japanese language?
2. How has Japanese business culture changed?

DISCUSSION. What do you think could be some positive and negative results of the changes described in the article?

TOP NOTCH INTERACTION • *Is change for the better?*

STEP 1. **Have cultural features changed a little or a lot in the last fifty years? Complete the survey.**

Culture Survey	have changed a little	have changed a lot	Is the change for the better? (YES or NO)	
1. Table manners	☐	☐	☐	☐
2. Musical tastes	☐	☐	☐	☐
3. Dating customs	☐	☐	☐	☐
4. Clothing customs	☐	☐	☐	☐
5. Rules about formal behavior	☐	☐	☐	☐
6. Rules about punctuality	☐	☐	☐	☐
7. Forms of address	☐	☐	☐	☐
8. Male / female roles in the workplace	☐	☐	☐	☐
9. Male / female roles in the home	☐	☐	☐	☐
			Total YES answers: ______	

Are you a dinosaur or a chameleon?

How many times did you check YES in the third column?

0–3 = Definitely a dinosaur. You prefer to stick with tradition. Your motto: "If it isn't broken, don't fix it!"

4–6 = A little of both. You're willing to adapt to change, but not too fast. Your motto: "Easy does it!"

7–9 = Definitely a chameleon. You adapt to change easily. Your motto: "Out with the old, in with the new!"

STEP 2. PAIR WORK. **Compare and discuss your answers and give specific examples of changes for each answer.**

"I think clothing customs have become less modest. My mother had to wear a uniform to school. But by the time I started school, girls had stopped wearing them. Now girls can go to school in jeans and even shorts!"

STEP 3. DISCUSSION.

- What are the advantages and disadvantages of the changes in your culture? Does everyone think change is good?
- Do older and younger people disagree about culture change? Do men and women disagree?

NEED HELP? **Here's language you already know:**

Agree about facts
[People don't use titles as much], do they?
[Clothing customs used to be more modest], didn't they?

Agree in general
I agree. I think you're right.

Disagree in general
I disagree.
Actually, I don't agree, because ___.
Really? I think ___.

Formality and informality
be on a first-name basis
prefer to be addressed by their first [last] names / titles and family names

UNIT **1**
CHECKPOINT

A LISTENING COMPREHENSION. Listen to the conversations of people introducing themselves. Check the statement in each pair that's true.

1. ☐ She'd like to be addressed by her title and family name.
   ☐ She'd like to be addressed by her first name.
2. ☐ She'd prefer to be called by her first name.
   ☐ She'd prefer to be called by her title and last name.
3. ☐ It's customary to call people by their first name there.
   ☐ It's not customary to call people by their first name there.
4. ☐ He's comfortable with the policy about names.
   ☐ He's not comfortable with the policy about names.
5. ☐ She prefers to use the title Mrs.
   ☐ She prefers to use the title Dr.

TOP NOTCH SONG
"It's a Great Day for Love"
Lyrics on last book page.

TOP NOTCH PROJECT
Make a cultural literacy guidebook. Find cultural information about countries you'd like to visit on the Internet.

TOP NOTCH WEBSITE
For Unit 1 online activities, visit the *Top Notch* Companion Website at www.longman.com/topnotch.

B Complete each statement with a tag question.

1. You're not from around here, ____________?
2. You were in this class last year, ____________?
3. They haven't been here since yesterday, ____________?
4. It's impolite to ask people their age, ____________?
5. These chrysanthemums are an OK gift here, ____________?
6. I met you on the tour in Nepal, ____________?
7. We'll have a chance to discuss this tomorrow, ____________?
8. By 10:00 he had already picked up her passport, ____________?

A chrysanthemum. Chrysanthemums are an inappropriate social gift in some countries.

C Complete each statement.

1. Behaving impolitely when eating with others is an example of bad ____________ .
2. Each country has customs and traditions about how to behave in social situations. The rules are sometimes called ____________ .
3. Each culture has its own sense of ____________ . It's important to understand people's ideas about lateness.

D WRITING. Is etiquette important? On a separate sheet of paper, explain your opinion. Include some or all of the words in the box.

impolite	polite	taboo
table manners	formal	informal

Unit Wrap-Up

- **Grammar.** Make statements with question tags about the picture.
  Machu Picchu is really interesting, isn't it?
- **Social Language.** Create conversations for the people on the tour.
  A: Do you mind if I call you Jane?
  B: Absolutely not. Please do.
- **Writing.** Write about the people in the picture.
  There are people from different cultures on the tour . . .

Now I can . . .

- ☐ meet someone and make small talk.
- ☐ get to know someone.
- ☐ be culturally literate.
- ☐ discuss how culture changes over time.

UNIT 2

Health Matters

UNIT GOALS

1 Make an appointment to see a dentist
2 Describe symptoms at a doctor's office
3 Discuss types of medical treatments
4 Talk about medications

TOPIC PREVIEW. Read the health checklist for international travelers. Which tips do you think are the most important?

Before you go...

A checklist for international travelers

Vaccinations

You may be required to get vaccinated before you are allowed to enter certain countries. Check the immunization requirements of the country you are visiting. The farther "off the beaten path" you travel, the more important it is to be protected from illness and disease.

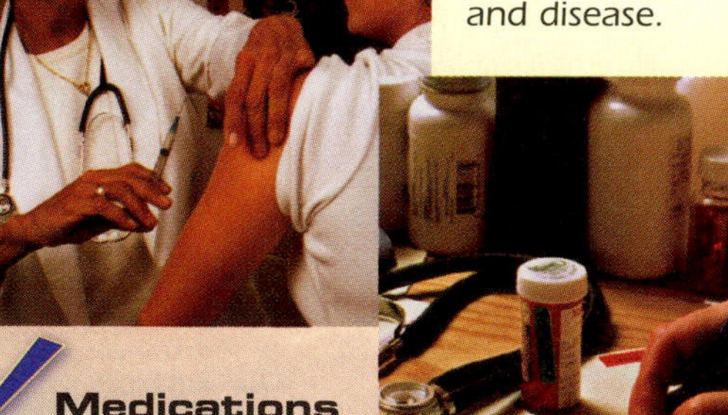

Medications

Talk to your doctor before your trip. Your doctor may be able to write a prescription for extra medication or give you tips for staying healthy while traveling. Buy and pack a supply of all medications you take regularly. Carry your medications in your carry-on bags. If you lose your luggage, you will still have them.

Eyewear

If you wear glasses or contact lenses, get a copy of your prescription before you go. Carry it with you in case you break or lose your eyewear. Or be sure to carry an extra pair with you.

Dental care

There's nothing more frightening than having a toothache when you're far from home. Have a dental check-up before you leave on a long trip to avoid any problems.

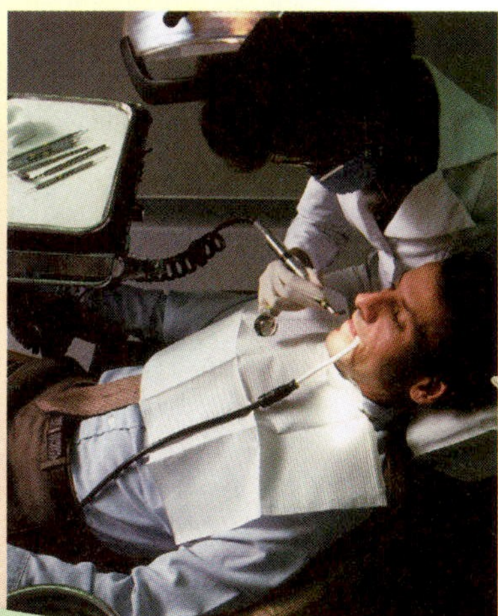

SOURCE: www.atevo.com

PAIR WORK. In addition to medical items, what else should go on a checklist for an international trip? Write a list with your partner.

CHECKLIST

☑ ______________________

☑ ______________________

☑ ______________________

☑ ______________________

C SOUND BITES. Read along silently as you listen to two short conversations in Russia.

GUEST: I need to see a dentist as soon as possible. I think it's an emergency. I was wondering if you might be able to recommend someone who speaks English.

CLERK: Actually, there's one not far from here. Would you like me to make an appointment for you?

DENTIST: So I hear you're from overseas.

PATIENT: Yes. From Venezuela. Thanks for fitting me in. This tooth is killing me.

DENTIST: Luckily, I had a cancellation. Glad to be of help.

PATIENT: I really appreciate it. Thought I'd better see someone right away.

DENTIST: Well, let's have a look.

D Check the statements that you are sure are true. Explain your answers.

☐ **1.** The hotel guest is having a dental emergency.

☐ **2.** The hotel guest is on vacation.

☐ **3.** The hotel clerk offers to call the dentist.

☐ **4.** It was easy to get an appointment with the dentist.

E IN OTHER WORDS. Explain the meaning of each underlined phrase.

1. "So <u>I hear</u> you're from overseas."
2. "Thanks for <u>fitting me in</u>."
3. "This tooth <u>is killing me</u>."
4. "Well, <u>let's have a look</u>."

WHAT ABOUT YOU?

Have you ever had a medical or dental emergency? Where were you? What happened? What did you do?

"Last year, I went skiing and I broke my arm. I had to go to the emergency room at the hospital."

LESSON 1

Make an Appointment to See a Dentist

CONVERSATION MODEL Read and listen.

A: Hello. I wonder if I might be able to see the dentist today. I'm here on business, and I have a toothache.

B: Oh, that must hurt. Are you in a lot of pain?

A: Yes, actually, I am.

B: Well, let me check. Could you be here by 3:00?

A: Yes. That would be fine. I really appreciate it.

Rhythm and intonation practice

A VOCABULARY. Dental emergencies. Listen and practice.

I have a toothache.

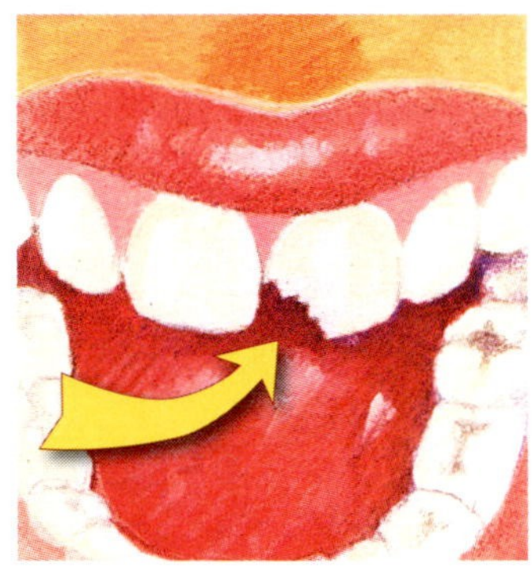

I broke a tooth.

I lost a filling.

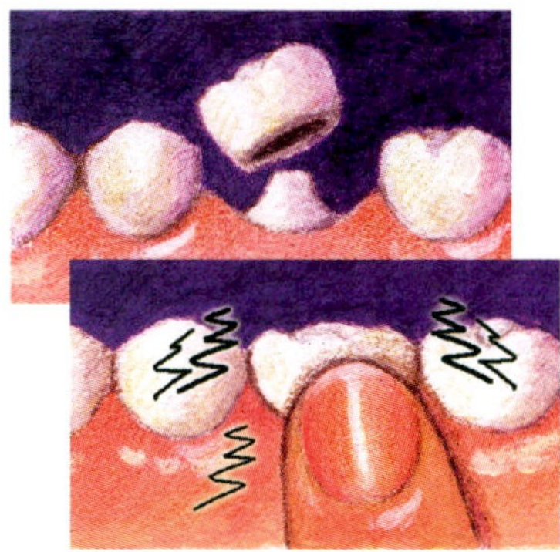

My crown is loose.

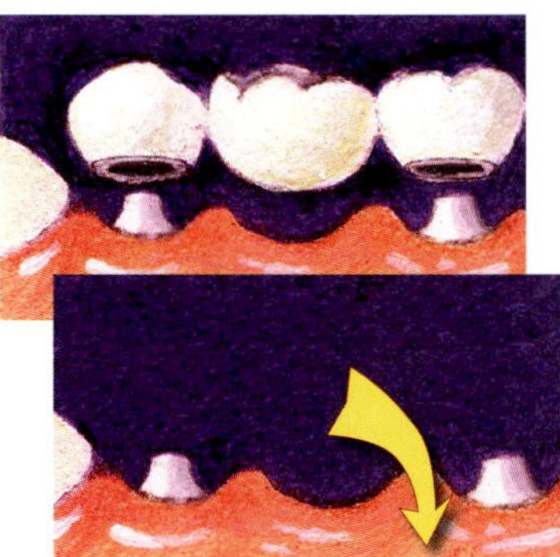

My bridge came out.

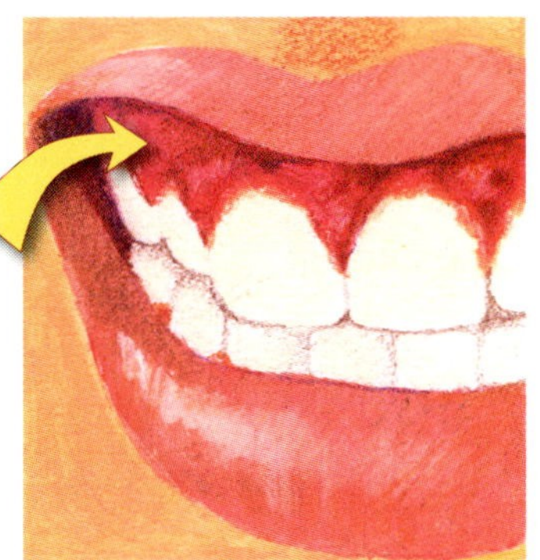

My gums are swollen.

B LISTENING COMPREHENSION. Listen to the conversations.

Complete each statement to describe the dental problem.

1. The man lost ______ .
2. The woman's ______ is loose.
3. The man's ______ came out.
4. The woman just broke ______ .

C GRAMMAR. May, might, must, and be able to

May or might for possibility

Use may or might and the base form to express possibility. They have the same meaning.

The dentist **may** (or **might**) **have** some time to see you.
Barbara **might** (or **may**) **not need** a new filling.

Must for conclusions

Use must and the base form of a verb when something is almost certainly true.

John just broke a tooth. That **must hurt**.
The dentist told me to come next week. It **must not be** an emergency.

Be able to for ability

Be able to has the same meaning as can.

She**'ll be able to see** you tomorrow. = She **can see** you tomorrow.

Note: You can use be able to or have to with may, might, or must.

Dr. Sharp	**may**	**be able to**	**help** you.
I	**might not**	**be able to**	**get** there till 6:00.
You	**might**	**have to**	**get** a new crown.
She	**must not**	**have to**	**go** to work today.

PAGE G3
For more ...

D PAIR WORK. Discuss the questions. Use may or might.

1. When will you practice English outside class this week?
2. When will you need to use English in your life?

E Complete the conversations by drawing conclusions with must or must not.

1. **A:** You look terrible! Your tooth _______ really hurt.
   B: It does.
2. **A:** Did you call the dentist?
   B: Yes, but no one is answering. The dentist _______ be in today.
3. **A:** Bill had a bad toothache this morning.
   B: No kidding. Then he _______ be able to come to the meeting today.
4. **A:** Where's Alice?
   B: Well, I heard she lost a filling, so she _______ be at the dentist.

CONVERSATION PAIR WORK

Role-play making an appointment to see a dentist. Start like this:

A: Hello. I wonder if I might be able to see the dentist today. ______.

B: ______ ...

LESSON 2

Describe Symptoms at a Doctor's Office

CONVERSATION MODEL Read and listen.

A: You must be Mr. Brown. You're here for a blood test, aren't you?
B: That's right.
A: And is anything bothering you today?
B: Well, actually, I've been coughing.
A: Really? Well, why don't you have a seat? I'll see if the doctor can see you.

Rhythm and intonation practice

A VOCABULARY. Symptoms. Listen and practice.

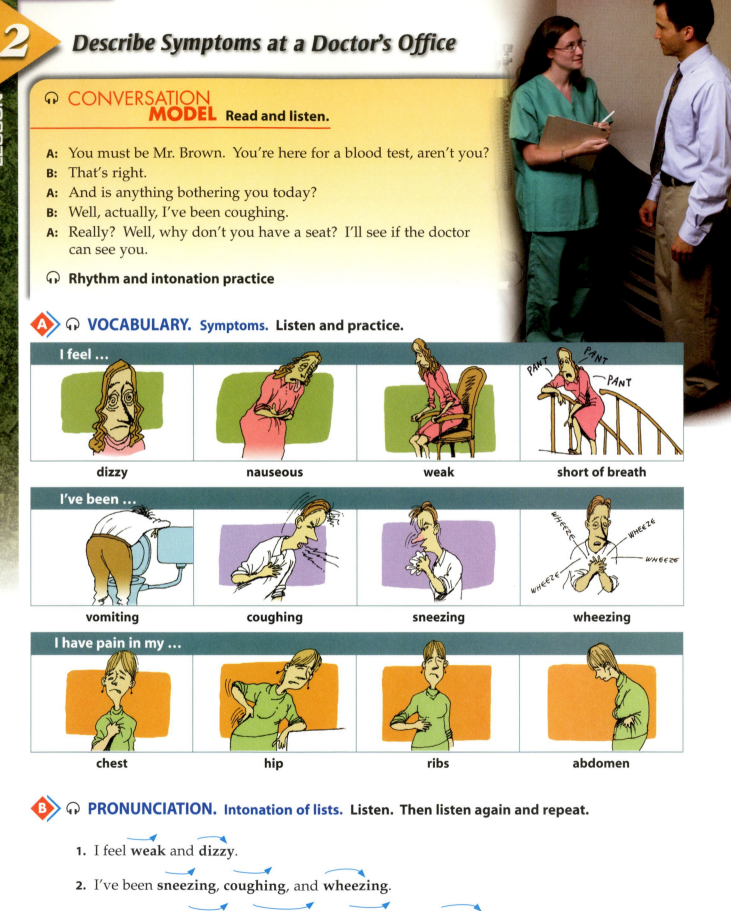

I feel …

dizzy | nauseous | weak | short of breath

I've been …

vomiting | coughing | sneezing | wheezing

I have pain in my …

chest | hip | ribs | abdomen

B PRONUNCIATION. Intonation of lists. Listen. Then listen again and repeat.

1. I feel **weak** and **dizzy**.
2. I've been **sneezing**, **coughing**, and **wheezing**.
3. I have pain in **my neck**, **my shoulders**, **my back**, and **my hip**.

C LISTENING COMPREHENSION. Listen to the conversations. Check the symptoms each patient describes. If the patient has any pain, where is it? Listen again to check your work.

	dizziness	nausea	weakness	vomiting	coughing	sneezing	wheezing	pain	if pain, where?
1.	☐	☐	☐	☐	☐	☐	☐	☐	
2.	☐	☐	☐	☐	☐	☐	☐	☐	
3.	☐	☐	☐	☐	☐	☐	☐	☐	
4.	☐	☐	☐	☐	☐	☐	☐	☐	
5.	☐	☐	☐	☐	☐	☐	☐	☐	
6.	☐	☐	☐	☐	☐	☐	☐	☐	

D VOCABULARY. Medical procedures. Listen and practice.

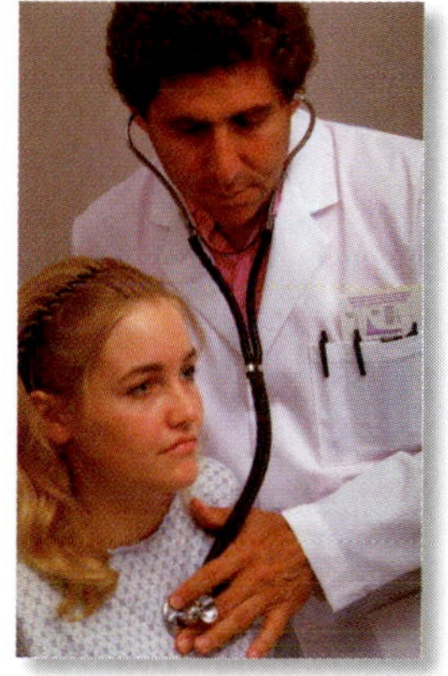
a checkup / an examination

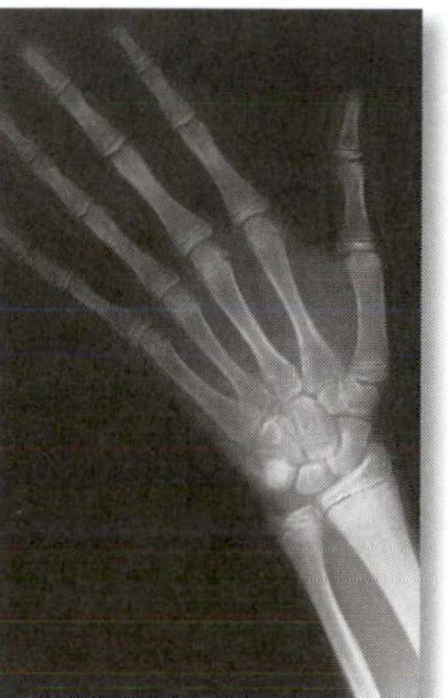
an X-ray

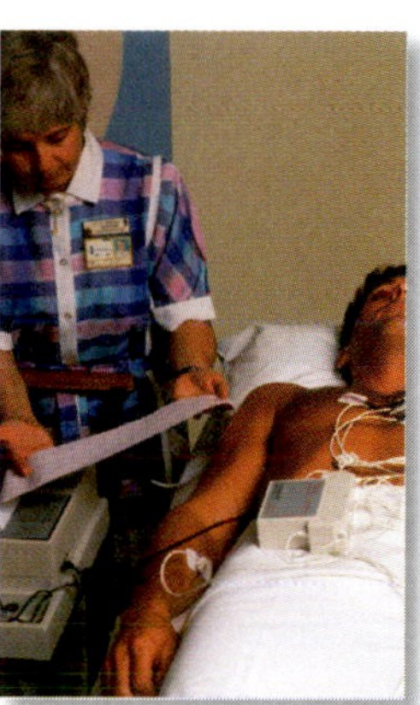
an EKG

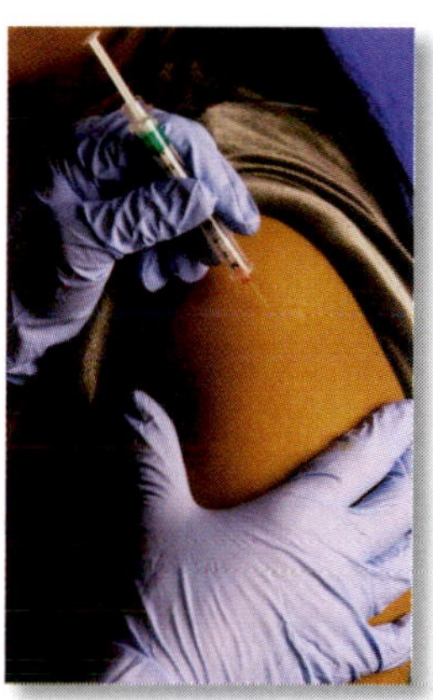
a shot / an injection

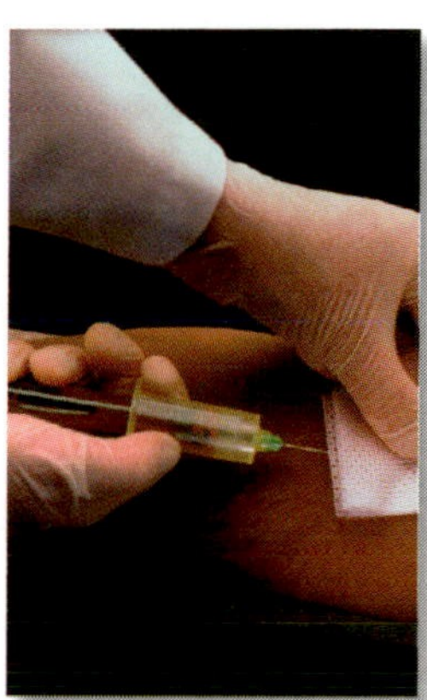
a blood test

CONVERSATION PAIR WORK

Role-play a visit to the doctor's office. Before you begin, choose a time and medical procedure and write it in the appointment book. Use the guide, or create a new conversation.

A: You must be _____. You're here for _____, aren't you?

B: _____.

A: And is anything bothering you today?

B: Well, actually, _____.

A: _____.

APPOINTMENTS

	patient's name	medical procedure
8:00		
9:00		
10:00		
11:00		
12:00		
1:00		
2:00		
3:00		
4:00		
5:00		
6:00		
7:00		

Discuss Types of Medical Treatments

LESSON

A READING WARM-UP. What do you do when you get sick or you're in pain?

B READING. Read the article. Which health treatments have you tried?

CONVENTIONAL MEDICINE

The beginnings of conventional medicine can be traced back to the fifth century B.C. in ancient Greece. It is based on the scientific study of the human body and illness. In the last century, there has been great progress in what doctors have been able to do with modern surgery and new medications. These scientific advances have made conventional medicine the method many people choose first when they need medical help.

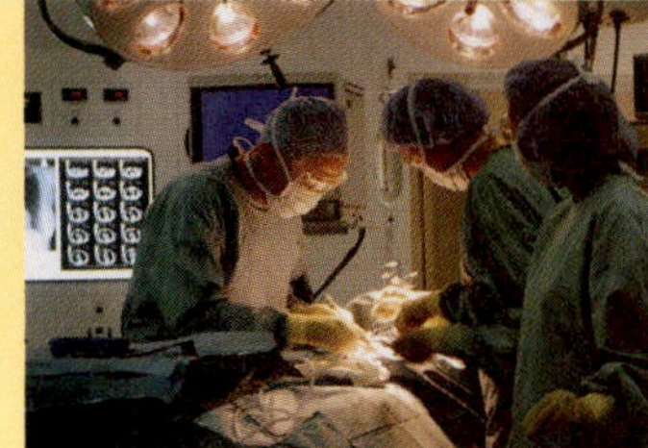

Surgical techniques have greatly improved over the last century.

Homeopathic remedies are popular in many countries.

HOMEOPATHY

Homeopathy was founded in the late eighteenth century in Germany. It is a low-cost system of natural medicine used by hundreds of millions of people worldwide, particularly in India, France, Germany, and the United Kingdom. Homeopathic remedies always come from plants and other natural sources, and they are designed to try to get the body to heal itself. The remedies are usually taken under the tongue.

HERBAL THERAPY

Herbal medicine, often taken as teas or pills, has been practiced for thousands of years in almost all cultures around the world. In fact, many conventional medicines were discovered by scientists studying traditional uses of herbs for medicinal purposes. The World Health Organization claims that 80% of the world's population uses some form of herbal therapy for their regular health care.

Herbs are used to treat many ailments.

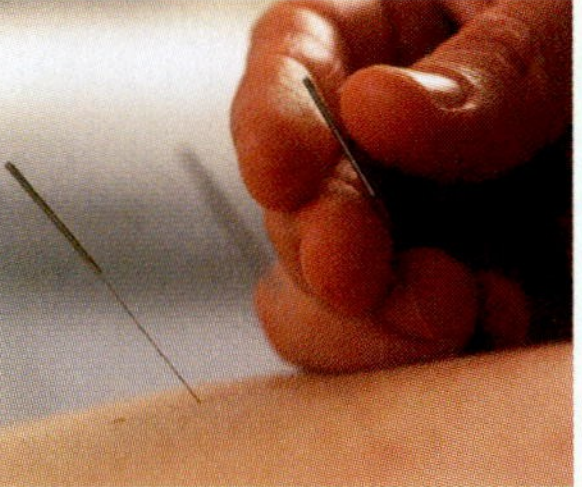

ACUPUNCTURE

Acupuncture originated in China over five thousand years ago. Today, it is used worldwide for a variety of problems. Acupuncture needles are inserted at certain points on the body to relieve pain and /or restore health. Many believe acupuncture may be effective in helping people stop smoking as well.

An acupuncturist inserts needles at certain points on the body.

CHIROPRACTIC

Chiropractic was introduced in the U.S. in 1895 and is now used by 15 million people worldwide for the treatment of pain, backache, injuries and some illnesses. Chiropractic uses no medications, but it is sometimes practiced along with herbal or homeopathic therapies.

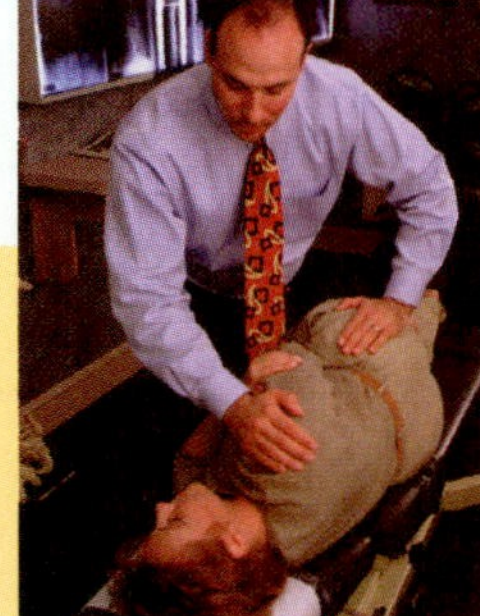

A chiropractor adjusts a patient's spine.

SPIRITUAL HEALING

Also known as faith healing, or mind and body connection, various forms of spiritual healing exist around the world. This is a form of healing that uses the mind or religious faith to treat illness. A number of conventional doctors even say that when they have not been able to help a patient, spiritual healing just may work.

Many believe meditation or prayer may help heal disease.

SOURCES: www.alternativemedicine.com and www.holisticmed.com

C DISCUSSION. Which of the treatments in the reading are available in your country? Which ones are the most popular? Why?

D WHAT DO YOU THINK? Match each patient to a treatment. Explain your answers. In some cases, more than one therapy might be appropriate.

1. "I want to avoid taking any strong medications or having surgery."

   This patient might prefer ____________.

2. "I believe you have to heal yourself. You can't just expect doctors to do everything for you."

   This patient might prefer ____________.

3. "I wouldn't use a health care method that isn't strongly supported by scientific research."

   This patient might prefer ____________.

TOP NOTCH INTERACTION • *What works for you?*

Practitioners
a conventional doctor
a homeopathic doctor
an acupuncturist
an herbal therapist
a chiropractor
a spiritual healer

STEP 1. PAIR WORK. Discuss the medical treatments and practitioners you would choose for each ailment. Take notes on your notepad.

	You	Your partner
a cold		
a headache		
nausea		
back pain		
a high fever		
a broken finger		

STEP 2. DISCUSSION. Compare the kinds of health care you and your classmates use. Explain why you use them.

"I've tried acupuncture a number of times. It really helped with my back pain."

"I would never try herbal medicine. I don't think it works."

"I see a homeopathic doctor regularly, but my husband doesn't believe in that."

STEP 3. WRITING. On a separate sheet of paper, write about the health care you use.

LESSON 4

Talk about Medications

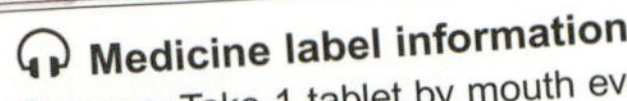

Medicine label information

Dosage: Take 1 tablet by mouth every day.
Warnings: Do not take this medication if you are pregnant or nursing a baby.
Side effects: May cause dizziness or nausea.

A VOCABULARY. Medications.

Listen and practice.

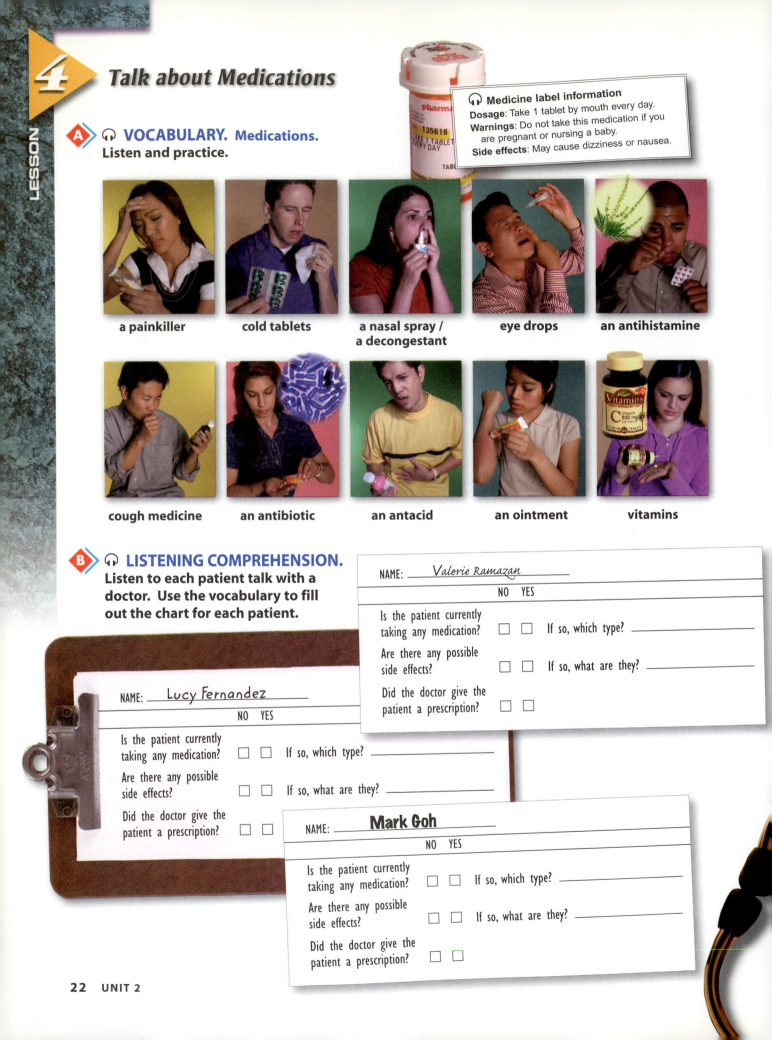

a painkiller

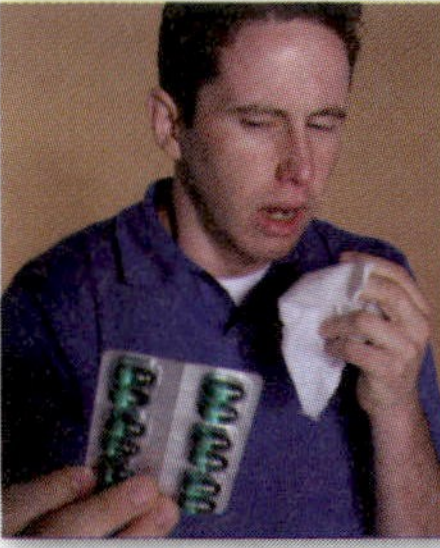

cold tablets

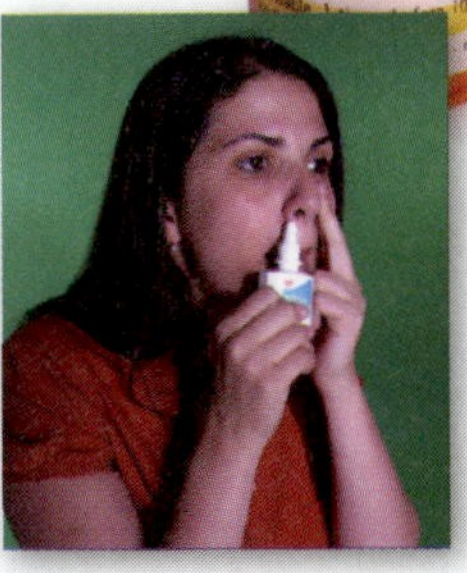

a nasal spray / a decongestant

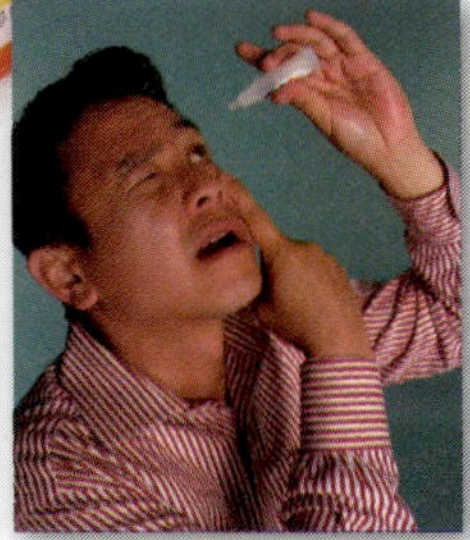

eye drops

an antihistamine

cough medicine

an antibiotic

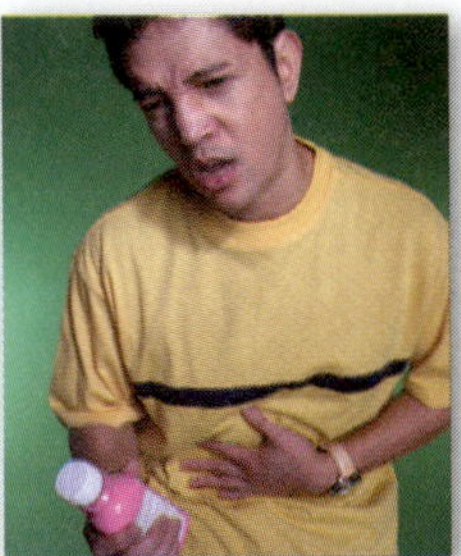

an antacid

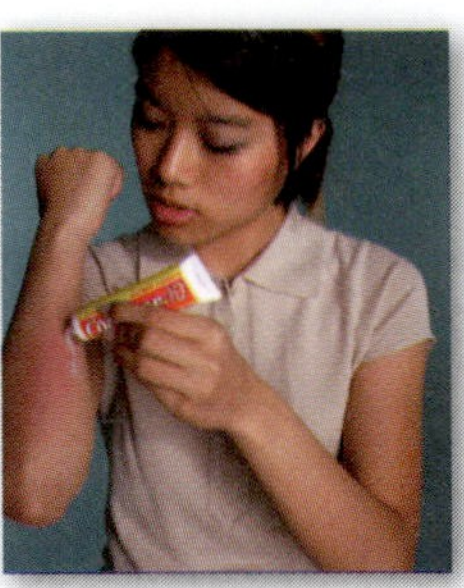

an ointment

vitamins

B LISTENING COMPREHENSION.

Listen to each patient talk with a doctor. Use the vocabulary to fill out the chart for each patient.

NAME: *Valerie Ramazan*

	NO	YES	
Is the patient currently taking any medication?	☐	☐	If so, which type? ______
Are there any possible side effects?	☐	☐	If so, what are they? ______
Did the doctor give the patient a prescription?	☐	☐	

NAME: *Lucy Fernandez*

	NO	YES	
Is the patient currently taking any medication?	☐	☐	If so, which type? ______
Are there any possible side effects?	☐	☐	If so, what are they? ______
Did the doctor give the patient a prescription?	☐	☐	

NAME: **Mark Goh**

	NO	YES	
Is the patient currently taking any medication?	☐	☐	If so, which type? ______
Are there any possible side effects?	☐	☐	If so, what are they? ______
Did the doctor give the patient a prescription?	☐	☐	

TOP NOTCH
INTERACTION • *Are you currently taking any medication?*

STEP 1. **Imagine you are visiting the doctor. Complete the patient information form.**

Patient Information Form

NAME: ____________________

1. What are your symptoms?
   - ☐ dizziness ☐ weakness ☐ shortness of breath
   - ☐ coughing ☐ sneezing ☐ wheezing
   - ☐ nausea ☐ vomiting ☐ pain (where?____)
   - ☐ other:__________
2. How long have you had these symptoms?__________
3. Are you currently taking any medications? If so, what?__________
4. Are you allergic to any medications? If so, which?__________

STEP 2. **ROLE PLAY.** **Take turns playing different roles. Use your patient information form. Include the following scenes:**

Roles
- a patient
- a colleague / classmate
- a doctor
- a receptionist

1. The colleague or classmate recommends a doctor.
2. The patient calls the receptionist to make an appointment.
3. The receptionist greets the patient at the office.
4. The doctor asks about the problem and suggests a treatment.

NEED HELP? **Here's language you already know:**

Finding a doctor

Could you recommend ___?

I'd like to make an appointment to see ___.

I think it's an emergency.

I really appreciate it.

At the doctor's office

Is it an emergency?

Why don't you have a seat?

You must be ___.

I'll see if the doctor can see you.

The doctor will be right with you.

The doctor

Luckily, I had a cancellation.

Glad I'm able to help you out.

It's a good idea to ___.

You should ___.

You may have to ___.

Let's have a look.

That must hurt.

The patient

Thanks for fitting me in.

My ___ is killing me.

I feel [dizzy].

I've been [coughing].

I have pain in my [ankle].

I thought I'd better see someone right away.

Are there any side effects?

UNIT 2 CHECKPOINT

A LISTENING COMPREHENSION. Listen to the conversations. Complete the statements.

1. The patient lost a ________.
2. The doctor wrote a prescription for an ________.
3. The doctor wants the patient to get an ________.
4. The patient wants to see an ________.

B Suggest a medication for each of the people.

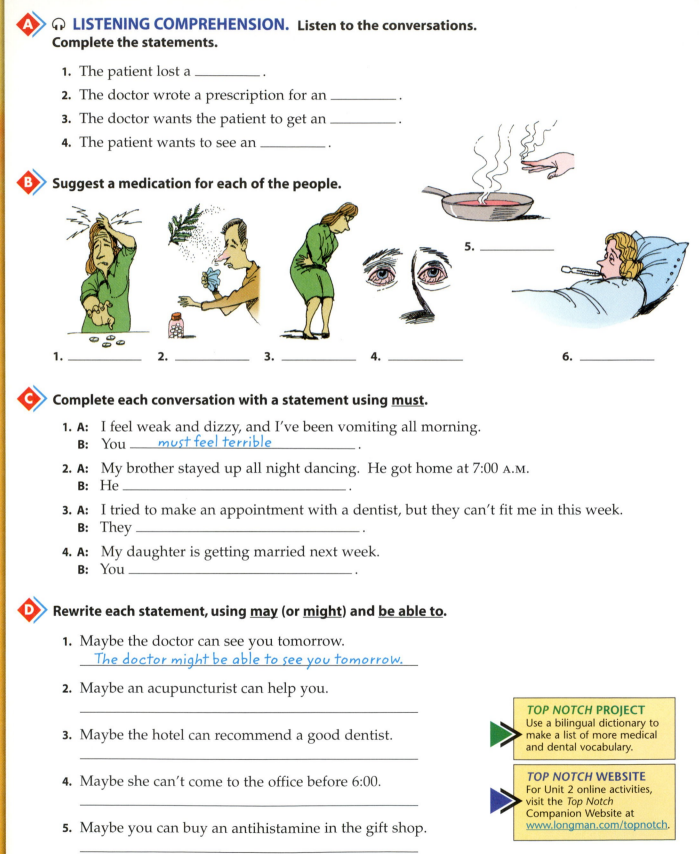

1. ________ 2. ________ 3. ________ 4. ________ 5. ________ 6. ________

C Complete each conversation with a statement using <u>must</u>.

1. **A:** I feel weak and dizzy, and I've been vomiting all morning.
   B: You _must feel terrible_.
2. **A:** My brother stayed up all night dancing. He got home at 7:00 A.M.
   B: He ________.
3. **A:** I tried to make an appointment with a dentist, but they can't fit me in this week.
   B: They ________.
4. **A:** My daughter is getting married next week.
   B: You ________.

D Rewrite each statement, using <u>may</u> (or <u>might</u>) and <u>be able to</u>.

1. Maybe the doctor can see you tomorrow.
   The doctor might be able to see you tomorrow.
2. Maybe an acupuncturist can help you.
   ____
3. Maybe the hotel can recommend a good dentist.
   ____
4. Maybe she can't come to the office before 6:00.
   ____
5. Maybe you can buy an antihistamine in the gift shop.
   ____

TOP NOTCH PROJECT
Use a bilingual dictionary to make a list of more medical and dental vocabulary.

TOP NOTCH WEBSITE
For Unit 2 online activities, visit the *Top Notch* Companion Website at www.longman.com/topnotch.

Unit Wrap-Up

- **Vocabulary.** Name all the treatments, procedures, and ailments you can see in the picture.
  backache, X-ray, . . .
- **Grammar.** Make statements with may or might and must.
  She must have a backache.
- **Social Language.** Create conversations for the people.
  A: I wonder if I might be able to see the dentist today.
  B: Is it an emergency?
- **Writing.** Write about what is happening in the picture.
  The medical office is very busy today. There are a lot of . . .

Now I can . . .

- ☐ make an appointment to see a doctor or dentist.
- ☐ describe symptoms at a doctor's office.
- ☐ discuss types of medical treatments.
- ☐ talk about medications.

UNIT 3

Getting Things Done

UNIT GOALS

1 Request express service
2 Ask for a recommendation
3 Evaluate the quality of service
4 Plan a social event

 **TOPIC PREVIEW.** Look at the business services website.

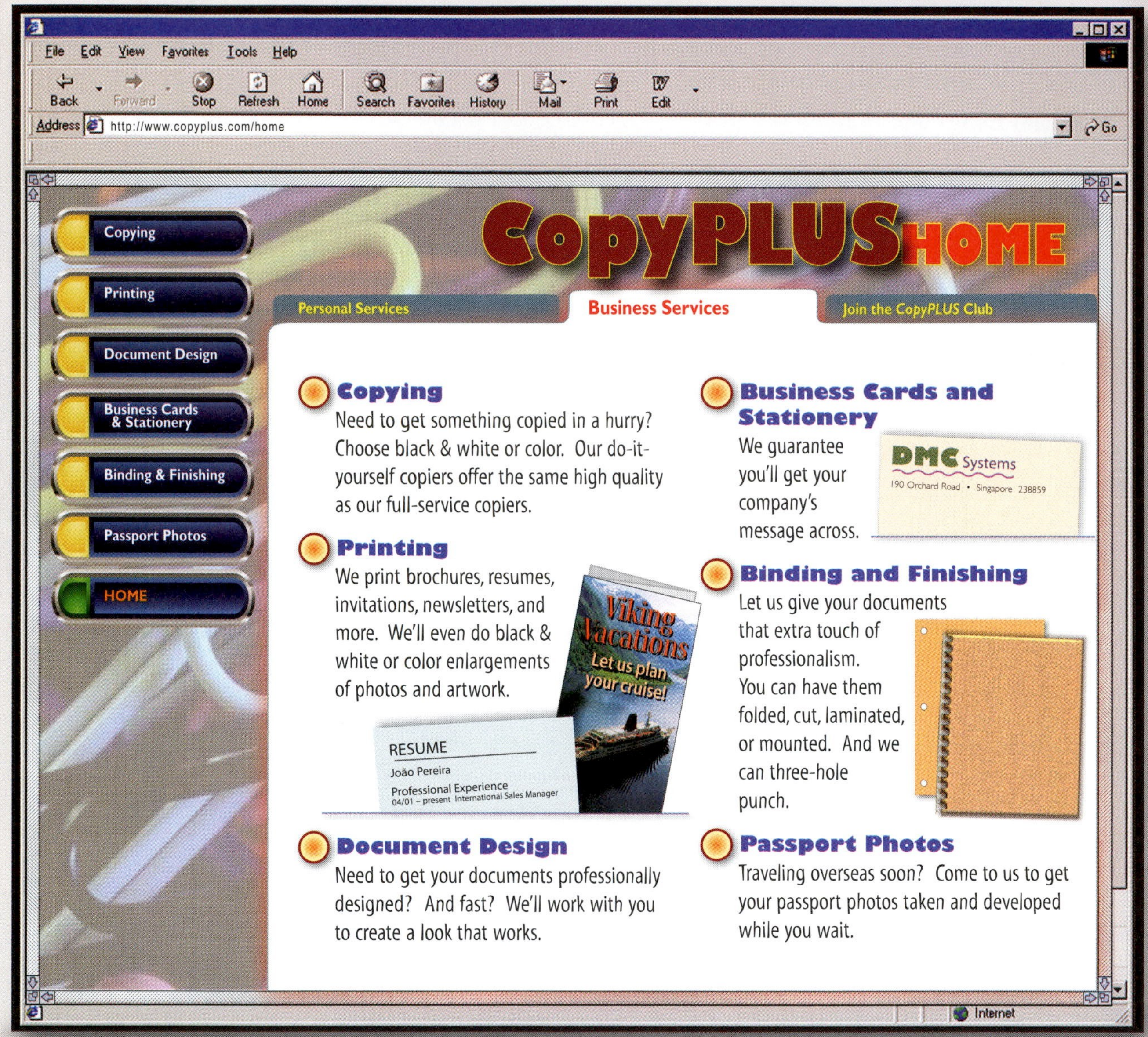

File Edit View Favorites Tools Help

Back Forward Stop Refresh Home Search Favorites History Mail Print Edit

Address http://www.copyplus.com/home

Copying
Printing
Document Design
Business Cards & Stationery
Binding & Finishing
Passport Photos
HOME

CopyPLUS HOME

Personal Services | Business Services | Join the CopyPLUS Club

Copying

Need to get something copied in a hurry? Choose black & white or color. Our do-it-yourself copiers offer the same high quality as our full-service copiers.

Printing

We print brochures, resumes, invitations, newsletters, and more. We'll even do black & white or color enlargements of photos and artwork.

Viking Vacations
Let us plan your cruise!
RESUME
João Pereira
Professional Experience
04/01 – present International Sales Manager

Document Design

Need to get your documents professionally designed? And fast? We'll work with you to create a look that works.

Business Cards and Stationery

We guarantee you'll get your company's message across.

Binding and Finishing

Let us give your documents that extra touch of professionalism. You can have them folded, cut, laminated, or mounted. And we can three-hole punch.

Passport Photos

Traveling overseas soon? Come to us to get your passport photos taken and developed while you wait.

Internet

 **DISCUSSION.** When might you need each of these services? Give examples.

"If I started my own business, I might want to print some brochures."

"If I travel overseas, I'll need a passport."

C SOUND BITES. Read along silently as you listen to a natural conversation.

SUE: You look like you're in a hurry!
KIM: I am. I've got to get 50 color copies made a.s.a.p.* I hope they can do a rush job.
SUE: They must get requests like that all the time.
KIM: I sure hope so. But that's not all.
SUE: What else?

*a.s.a.p. = as soon as possible

KIM: Then I've got to get it all air expressed so it arrives in Singapore first thing Monday morning.
SUE: I won't keep you then. Actually, I'm in a bit of a hurry myself. I need to have the tailor put new buttons on this jacket.
KIM: OK. I'll call you tonight.
SUE: Great!

D IN OTHER WORDS. Read the conversation again and restate the following underlined words and phrases in your <u>own</u> way.

1. You look like you're <u>in a hurry</u>.
2. I hope they can <u>do a rush job</u>.
3. <u>first thing</u> Monday morning
4. I <u>won't keep you</u> then.

WHAT ABOUT YOU?

PAIR WORK. Which business and non-business services have you used in the last year? Who was the service provider? Which other services have you used?

☐ copying

☐ printing

☐ housecleaning

☐ car repair

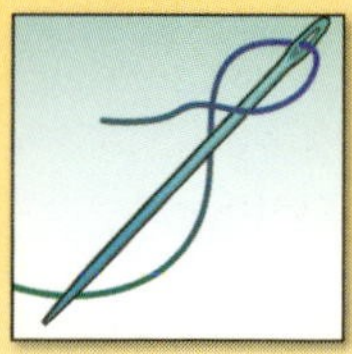
☐ tailoring

☐ courier service

LESSON 1

Request Express Service

CONVERSATION MODEL Read and listen.

A: Do you think I could get this dry-cleaned by Thursday?
B: Thursday? That might be difficult.
A: I'm sorry, but it's pretty urgent. I need it for a friend's wedding this weekend.
B: Well, in that case, I'll see what I can do. But it won't be ready until after four o'clock.
A: I really appreciate it. Thanks.

Rhythm and intonation practice

VOCABULARY. Services. Listen and practice.

dry-clean a suit

develop / process film

repair shoes

frame a picture

deliver a package

lengthen / shorten a skirt

enlarge photos

print a sign

copy a report

B GRAMMAR. The passive causative

Use get or have with an object and the past participle to talk about arranging services. Get and have have the same meaning in the passive causative.

	get / have	object	past participle	
They	got	their vacation photos	enlarged.	
I need to	get	this report	copied.	
We	're having	the office	cleaned	tomorrow.
She can	have	her film	developed	in an hour.

A by phrase is used when the speaker thinks that information is important.

We're having the office cleaned **by Royal Cleaning Services**.

They got the copier repaired yesterday. (no by phrase; not necessary to know by whom)

PAGE G4
For more ...

C LISTENING COMPREHENSION. Listen to the conversations. Complete each statement with the item and a service.

1. He wants to get his ________ ________.
2. She needs to get her ________ ________.
3. He needs to have his ________ ________.
4. She wants to have a ________ ________.

D Use the cues to write questions with the passive causative.

1. Would it be possible to / these pictures / frame / by next week? ________________
2. Could I / these shoes / repair / here? ________________
3. Can I / this shirt / dry-clean / by tomorrow? ________________
4. Where can I / these gloves / gift wrap? ________________
5. Is it possible to / these photos / enlarge / before 5:00? ________________

E PAIR WORK. Where do you go for these services? Use the passive causative.

dry-clean clothes
cut hair
process film
make photocopies
repair shoes

"Where do you get your clothes dry-cleaned?"

"I usually get them dry-cleaned at ..."

CONVERSATION PAIR WORK

Role-play asking for express service.

A: Do you think I could _____ by _____?
B: _____? That might be difficult.
A: _____ ...

Continue the conversation in your own way.

Ideas for why you might be in a rush:
for a wedding
for a business trip
for a vacation
for a new job

LESSON

Ask for a Recommendation

CONVERSATION MODEL Read and listen.

A: I have to get this to Chicago a.s.a.p. Can you recommend a courier service?
B: Why don't you have Aero Flash take care of it?
A: Have you used them before?
B: Sure. They're really reliable. And they can deliver a package anywhere in the world in two business days.

Rhythm and intonation practice

A GRAMMAR. Causatives get, have, and make

Use the causative to show that one person causes another person to do something. With get, use an object and an infinitive. With have, use an object and a base form of a verb.

		object	infinitive	
I	**got**	my brother	**to help**	me finish the job.
		object	**base form**	
She	**had**	her assistant	**plan**	the meeting.

To suggest an obligation, use make with an object and a base form.
I **made** my brother **help** me finish the job.

PAGES G4–G5
For more ...

B Correct the error in each sentence.

1. Why don't you have your assistant ~~to~~ call them?
2. Why didn't you get your sister help you?
3. I'll never be able to get the dry cleaner do this by tomorrow!
4. You should have the hotel to give you your money back.
5. Why don't you make your brother to wash the dishes?
6. I'm sure we can get the store process the film in an hour.

C VOCABULARY. Adjectives to describe services. Listen and practice.

reliable can be trusted to keep a promise
reasonable doesn't charge too much money
fast does the job in a short time
honest does not lie or cheat
efficient doesn't waste time
helpful is willing to help
professional does a very good job

PRONUNCIATION. Emphatic stress to express enthusiasm. Listen and repeat.

1. They're **REALly** reliable.
2. They're **inCREDibly** fast.
3. He's **exTREMEly** helpful.
4. She's **SO** professional.

Circle the best adjective for each situation.

1. "Link Copy Service was so (reasonable / helpful / honest). They delivered the job to my office before I had to leave for the airport."
2. "I find Portello's to be extremely (professional / fast / reasonable). I've shopped around and I can't find another service with such low prices."
3. "If you're looking for a good housecleaning service, I'd recommend Citywide Services. They're incredibly (efficient / reliable / honest). They have two people working together to complete the job in no time at all."
4. "What I like about Dom's Auto Service is that they're so (fast / reasonable / honest). There are so many other places that you can't trust. But at Dom's they always tell you the truth."

CONVERSATION PAIR WORK

Role-play asking for a recommendation. Use the guide and the ads, or create your own conversation.

A: I have to ____ a.s.a.p. Can you recommend a ____?
B: Why don't you have ____ take care of it?
A: Have you used them before?
B: ____ …

Continue the conversation in your own way.

Ideas:

- You need someone to make 200 color copies of a report.
- You need someone to send a package to Moscow.
- You need someone to dry–clean your suit / dress / jacket before an important meeting.
- You need someone to service your car before a long trip.

a copy service

a courier service

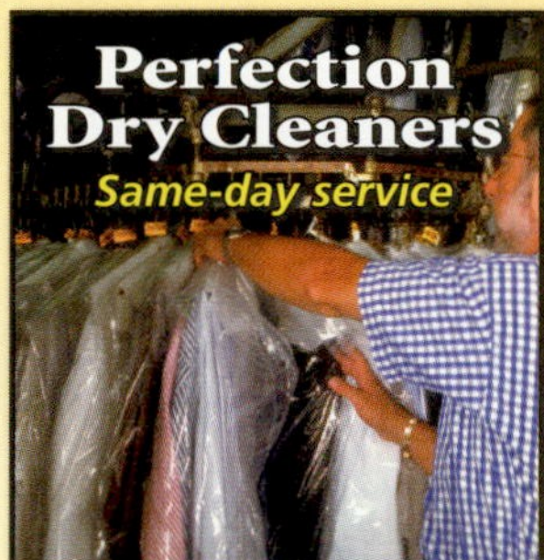

a dry cleaner

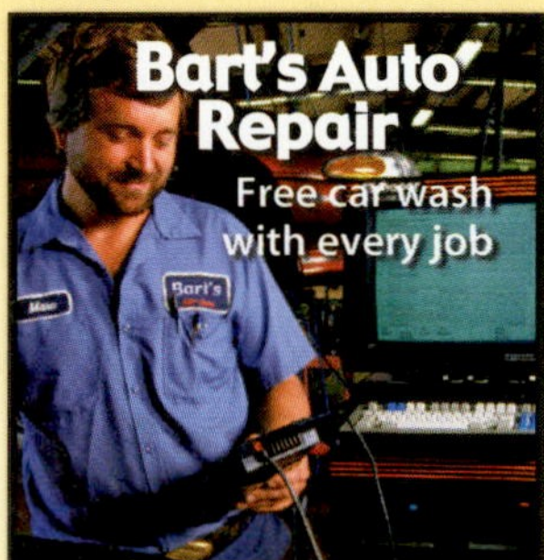

an auto repair shop

CONTROLLED PRACTICE

Evaluate the Quality of Service

A READING WARM-UP. **Have you ever bought handmade clothing or other handmade things? Do you prefer handmade or factory-made?**

B READING. **Read the tourist information for visitors to Hong Kong. Are there services like these in your city or town?**

PLACES TO SHOP

HONG KONG TAILORS

The famous Hong Kong 24-hour suit is a thing of the past, but you can still have clothes custom-made in a few days. Today, prices are no longer as low as they once were, but they're often about what you'd pay for a ready-made garment back home; the difference, of course, is that a tailor-made garment should fit you perfectly. The workmanship and quality of the better established shops rival even those of London's Savile Row—at less than half the price. A top-quality men's suit will run about HK$7,000 (US$910) or more, including fabric, while a silk shirt can cost HK$600 (US$78).

You can choose from a variety of fabrics.

Tailors in Hong Kong will make almost any garment you want—suits, evening gowns, wedding dresses, leather jackets, even monogrammed shirts. Many tailors offer a wide range of cloth from which to choose, from cotton and linen to very fine wools, cashmere, and silk. Hong Kong tailors are excellent at copying fashions. Bring a picture or drawing of what you want.

You should allow three to five days to have a garment custom-made, with at least two or three fittings. If you aren't satisfied during the fittings, speak up. Alterations should be included in the original price. If, in the end, you still don't like the finished product, you don't have to accept it. However, you will forfeit the deposit you are required to pay before the tailor begins working, usually about 50% of the total cost.

At your first fitting, the tailor will take your measurements. At your next fitting, the tailor will make alterations until you're satisfied.

With more than 2,500 tailoring establishments in Hong Kong, it shouldn't be any problem finding one. Some of the most famous are located in hotel shopping arcades and shopping complexes, but the more upscale the location, the higher the prices.

You can get anything made—from an evening gown to a monogrammed shirt.

Once you've had something custom-made and your tailor has your measurements, you will more than likely be able to order additional clothing later, even after you've returned home!

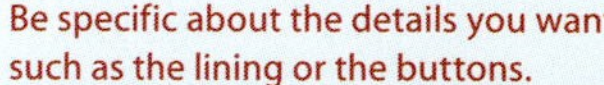

Be specific about the details you want, such as the lining or the buttons.

SOURCE: *Frommer's Hong Kong*, 7th edition

C PAIR WORK. **Check the statements that are true, according to the article. Find the information to support your answers in the reading.**

- ☐ **1.** You used to be able to get a suit made in 24 hours in Hong Kong.
- ☐ **2.** If you buy a ready-made garment at a store at home, it will cost about the same as a custom-made garment in Hong Kong.
- ☐ **3.** If you get a garment made on Savile Row, you will pay about 50 percent less than you would pay for the same garment made in Hong Kong.
- ☐ **4.** If you don't like the garment you ordered, you can get all your money back.
- ☐ **5.** If you want to pay a low price for a custom-made garment, go to an upscale hotel shopping arcade.

D DISCUSSION. **Do you think the Hong Kong tailoring services described in the tour guide sound like "a good deal"? What's more important to you—price or quality?**

TOP NOTCH INTERACTION • *They're the best!*

STEP 1. **What services do you use? Complete the chart. Write the name of the business, and check the reasons why you use that service. Then compare your chart with your partner's.**

	name of business	speed	reliability	price	workmanship	location
dry cleaning		☐	☐	☐	☐	☐
photo processing		☐	☐	☐	☐	☐
auto repair		☐	☐	☐	☐	☐
bicycle repair		☐	☐	☐	☐	☐
tailoring		☐	☐	☐	☐	☐
express delivery		☐	☐	☐	☐	☐
shoe repair		☐	☐	☐	☐	☐
hair stylist		☐	☐	☐	☐	☐
other:		☐	☐	☐	☐	☐

STEP 2. DISCUSSION. **Recommend local businesses to your classmates. Explain why you use them.**

"I always get my clothes dry-cleaned at Royal Dry Cleaners on 45th Road. They're really fast, and the prices are quite reasonable."

STEP 3. WRITING. **Write an advertisement for a local service that you use and like. Describe the quality of the service and the workmanship.**

LESSON

Plan a Social Event

A **VOCABULARY. Steps for planning a social event. Listen and practice.**

make a guest list

pick a date, time, and place

make a budget

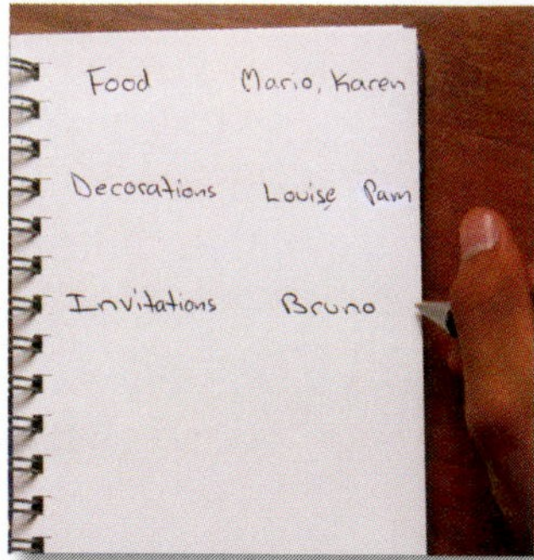

assign responsibilities

send out invitations

call a caterer

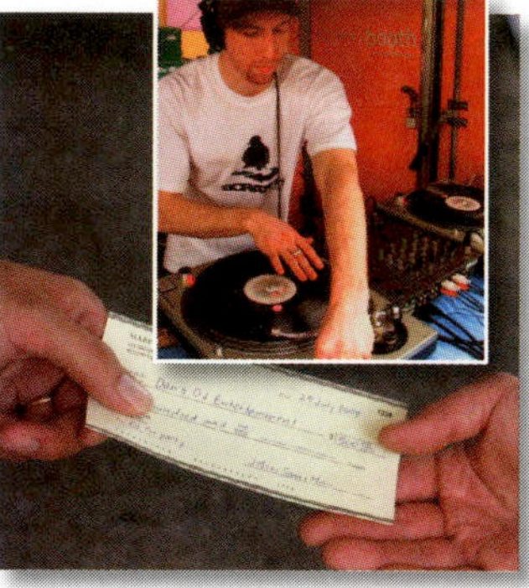
hire a DJ

decorate the room

B **LISTENING COMPREHENSION. Listen to the conversation. Number the steps in order. Then listen again and check who will do each step.**

	She'll do it herself.	She'll get help.
____ make a guest list	☐	☐
____ pick a date and time	☐	☐
____ pick a place	☐	☐
____ make a budget	☐	☐
____ assign responsibilities	☐	☐
____ send out invitations	☐	☐
____ call a caterer	☐	☐
____ hire a DJ	☐	☐
____ decorate the room	☐	☐

TOP NOTCH
INTERACTION • *Let's party!*

STEP 1. **Take the survey. Compare your answers with a partner's.**

What kind of personality do you have?

Check which activities you would rather do. Choose from column A or column B.

Column A		Column B
○ spend money	or	○ plan a budget
○ assign responsibility	or	○ take responsibility
○ design invitations	or	○ send invitations
○ play your own music	or	○ hire a DJ
○ decorate a room	or	○ make a guest list
○ bring your own food	or	○ call a caterer
○ dance	or	○ watch other people dance
○ sing	or	○ listen to other people sing
○ hire someone to clean	or	○ clean up after a party

If you chose:

five or more from column A,
you're the wild and creative type! You'd be a lot of fun at a party!

five or more from column B,
you're a born leader! You could plan a great party!

about the same from each column,
you're the best of both worlds!

Some ideas:

An end-of-year party? A birthday party? A TGIF* party?

*Thank Goodness It's Friday!

A talent show? A karaoke party?

An English practice day?

STEP 2. **GROUP WORK.** **Plan a social event for your class. Choose a type of event and discuss the steps you would need to take. Write the actions in your notepad.**

Type of event:

Steps:

UNIT 3 CHECKPOINT

A **LISTENING COMPREHENSION.** **Listen to each conversation. Write a sentence to describe what the customer needs and when.**

1. She needs to get her dress dry-cleaned by Friday.
2. ______________________
3. ______________________
4. ______________________

B **Complete each statement or question with a noun. Use your own words.**

1. Can I get my ____________ dry-cleaned here?
2. I'd like to have these ____________ lengthened.
3. Where can I get these ____________ shortened?
4. Can you tell me where I can get some ____________ copied?
5. Where did she get her ____________ framed?
6. How much did he pay to have his ____________ repaired?
7. I need to get some ____________ printed.
8. I'm in a hurry to have my ____________ processed.

C **Complete each causative statement in your own way. Begin with the base form of a verb or an infinitive.**

1. I got the teacher to help me with my writing ____________.
2. At the end of the meal, I had the waiter ____________.
3. Before my last vacation, I got the travel agent ____________.
4. When I was young, my mother always made me ____________.
5. When you arrive, you should get the hotel ____________.
6. Don't forget to have the gas station attendant ____________.
7. If you come for dinner, I promise I won't make you ____________.
8. Sad movies always make me ____________.
9. Maybe you can get your friend ____________.
10. You should have Air Express Courier Service ____________.

D **WRITING.** **What kinds of services are difficult to find? Write about the services you would like to have in your neighborhood.**

***TOP NOTCH* SONG**
"I'll Get Back to You"
Lyrics on last book page.

***TOP NOTCH* PROJECT**
Have a real social event for the class. Invite other classes to join you.

***TOP NOTCH* WEBSITE**
For Unit 3 online activities, visit the *Top Notch* Companion Website at www.longman.com/topnotch.

UNIT WRAP-UP

- **Social Language.** Create conversations for the people.
  I've got to get this to Los Angeles a.s.a.p.
- **Grammar.** Use the passive causative to describe the services the man wants or needs.
- **Writing.** Tell the story of the man's day.

Now I can ...

- ☐ request express service.
- ☐ ask for a recommendation.
- ☐ evaluate the quality of service.
- ☐ plan a social event.

UNIT 4

Life Choices

UNIT GOALS

1 Explain a change in life and work choices
2 Express regrets about decisions
3 Discuss skills, abilities, and qualifications
4 Discuss work and life decisions

A TOPIC PREVIEW. **Take the work preference inventory. Check the activities you would like to do.**

- ☐ work on experiments in a science laboratory
- ☐ write songs
- ☐ manage a department of a large business corporation
- ☐ repair furniture
- ☐ be a doctor and care for sick people
- ☐ design the stage scenery for a play
- ☐ teach adults how to read
- ☐ study a company's sales
- ☐ restore antique cars
- ☐ teach science to young people
- ☐ take a creative writing class
- ☐ read to blind people
- ☐ manage a company's sales representatives
- ☐ make clothes to sell
- ☐ interpret X-rays and other medical tests
- ☐ make paintings and sculptures
- ☐ help couples with marriage problems
- ☐ start my own business
- ☐ build houses

Write the number of check marks you have by each color.

	Field
☐	business
☐	science
☐	social work
☐	arts
☐	crafts

B DISCUSSION. **Which field did you have the most check marks for? What are some jobs in that field? Do you have a job in that field now? Would you like to? Is that job the same job you wanted when you were younger?**

C SOUND BITES. Read along silently as you listen to a natural conversation.

ANN: Ruth! This report's due tomorrow. What are you dreaming about?

RUTH: You know, I wish I'd gone to medical school instead of business school.

ANN: What? Since when have you been interested in medicine?

RUTH: Well, when I read about doctor shortages and terrible diseases, I think about how I could have made a difference in this world, an important difference… instead of doing these useless reports!

ANN: Well, you're young. Maybe it's not too late.

RUTH: Think so?

ANN: Sure. But do you think maybe you could get your head out of the clouds and get back on task now?

RUTH: Sorry about that. You can count on me.

D Check the statements that are true.

- ☐ **1.** Ann is surprised to hear about Ruth's interest in medicine.
- ☐ **2.** Ruth thinks business is more useful than medicine.
- ☐ **3.** Ruth would like to be a doctor.
- ☐ **4.** Ann suggests that it's possible for Ruth to change careers.

E IN OTHER WORDS. With a partner, restate each of the following statements in another way.

1. "I could have made a difference in this world…"
2. "Maybe it's not too late."
3. "…could [you] get your head out of the clouds and get back on task now?"
4. "You can count on me."

WHAT ABOUT **YOU?**

What regrets do you have in your life? What decisions do you wish you could change?

- ☐ a job choice
- ☐ a job change
- ☐ your studies
- ☐ your marriage / divorce
- ☐ a friendship that ended
- ☐ other: ______________

LESSON

1 Explain a Change in Life and Work Choices

CONVERSATION MODEL Read and listen.

A: Hey, Art! Long time no see.
B: Ben! How have you been?
A: Not bad, thanks. So what are you doing these days?
B: Well, I'm in dental school.
A: No kidding! I thought you had other plans.
B: That's right. I was going to be an artist, but I changed my mind.
A: How come?
B: Well, it's hard to make a living as a painter!

Rhythm and intonation practice

A GRAMMAR. Future in the past: was / were going to and would

Use was / were going to + the base form of a verb to express future plans someone had in the past.

I **was going to get** married, but I changed my mind.
I believed I **was going to have** a lot of children, but I was wrong.

Weren't you **going to study** law?	Yes, I was. / No, I wasn't.
Who **was going to teach** this class?	My sister was.
Where **were they going to study**?	In Prague.

Would + the base form of the verb can also express future in the past, but only after statements of knowledge or belief.

She thought she **would be** a doctor, but she changed her mind.
We always believed they **would get** married, but they never did.

PAGES G5–G7
For more ...

B Read each person's New Year's resolution from January 2000, the turn of the century. Write what each person was going to do.

Ivan Potok

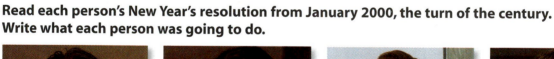

"I'm going to stop smoking."

Ivan was going to stop smoking.

Marie Duclos

"I'm going to apply to law school."

____

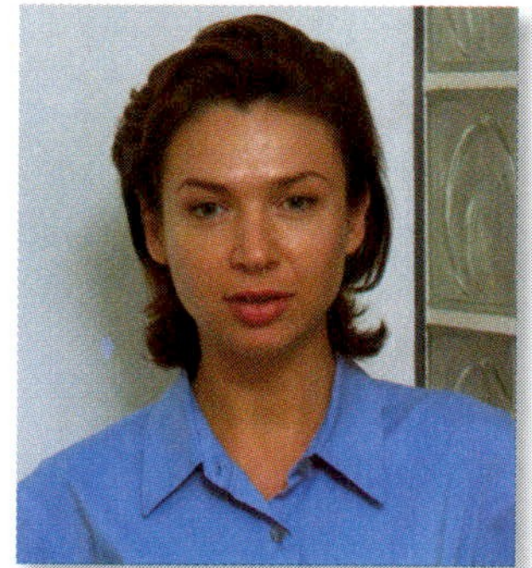

Sylvia Strook

"I'm going to find a husband."

____

Robert Park

"I'm going to marry Sylvia Strook."

____

C Use the cues to make statements with <u>would</u>.

1. In 1990 Sam thought / be / a lawyer, but he decided against it.
2. When I was young, I believed / study Chinese, but I never did.
3. Everyone was sure / Bill and Stella / get a divorce, but they didn't!
4. We didn't know / we / have so many children, but now we have six!

D **DISCUSSION.** Compare the plans and beliefs you had about your own future when you were young.

"When I was young, I thought I would be a teacher."

"That's amazing! I thought I was going to be a teacher too, but I changed my mind."

E **VOCABULARY.** Reasons for changing your mind. Listen and practice.

I wanted to be a rock star, but **my tastes changed**.

I was going to be an artist, but **it's hard to make a living as an artist**.

I thought I would be a lawyer, but **I didn't pass the exam**.

I wanted to be a firefighter, but **my family talked me out of it**.

I was going to marry George, but **I just changed my mind**.

F **LISTENING COMPREHENSION.** Listen to the conversations. Then listen again. Write the reason each person changed his or her mind.

Reason	
1. *It was hard to make a living as a sculptor.*	3.
2.	4.

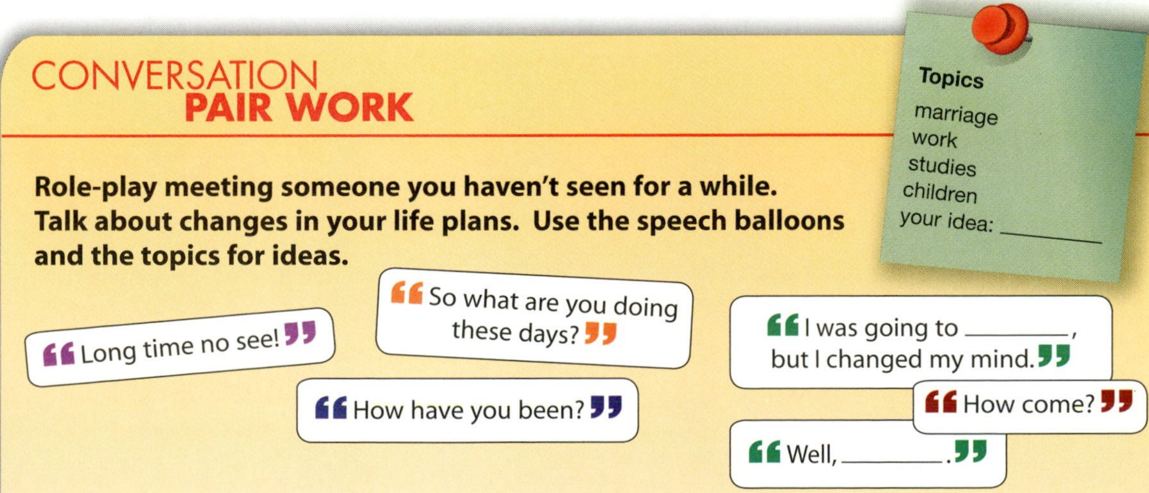

CONVERSATION **PAIR WORK**

Role-play meeting someone you haven't seen for a while. Talk about changes in your life plans. Use the speech balloons and the topics for ideas.

Topics
marriage
work
studies
children
your idea: ________
"Long time no see!"
"So what are you doing these days?"
"How have you been?"
"I was going to ________, but I changed my mind."
"How come?"
"Well, ________."

CONTROLLED **PRACTICE**

LESSON

2 Express Regrets about Decisions

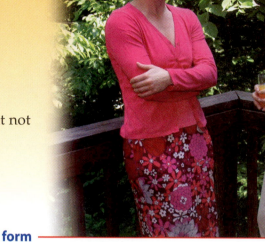

CONVERSATION MODEL Read and listen.

A: I should have married Steven.
B: Why do you think that?
A: Well, I might have had children by now.
B: Could be. But you never know. You might not have been happy.
A: True.

Rhythm and intonation practice

A GRAMMAR. Perfect modals: meaning and form

Express regrets about past actions with should have and a past participle.

I **should have studied** medicine. (But unfortunately, I didn't.)
She **shouldn't have divorced** Sam. (But unfortunately, she did.)

Speculate about the past with would have, could have, may have, and might have, and a past participle.

I should have married her. We **would have been** happy.
He **could have made** a better career choice.
I **may have failed** the entrance exam. It was very hard.
He **may** (or **might**) not **have been** able to make a living as a painter.

Draw conclusions about the past with must have and a past participle.

He's not here. He **must have gone** home early. (Probably—but I don't know for sure.)
They didn't buy the house. The price **must not have been** acceptable. (Probably—but I don't know for sure.)

PAGE G7
For more ...

B PAIR WORK. Share your regrets.

Partner A: Tell your partner what you regret about your life, your studies, your work, or your actions in the past. Use should have or shouldn't have.

Partner B: Ask why or why not.

"I should have studied architecture."
"Why?"
"I would have been a great architect!"

C 🎧 **PRONUNCIATION. Reduction of <u>have</u> in perfect modals. Listen to the reduction of <u>have</u> in perfect modals. Then repeat.**

1. I should have married Marie. (/ʃʊţəv/)
2. They might have left. (/maiţəv/)
3. We may not have seen it. (/naţəv/)
4. She could have been on time. (/cʊţəv/)

D **PAIR WORK. Provide reasons for each of the following statements.**
Partner A: Speculate with <u>may have</u> / <u>may not have</u> or <u>might have</u> / <u>might not have</u>.
Partner B: Draw a conclusion with <u>must have</u> or <u>must not have</u>.

Example: John is late for dinner.

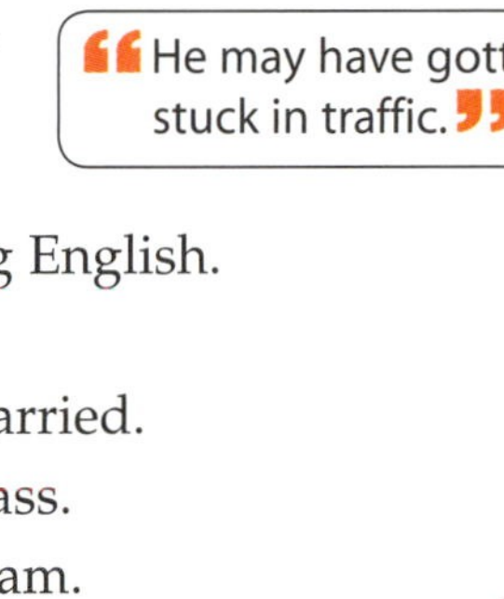

"He may have gotten stuck in traffic."
"He must have forgotten."

1. My brother stopped studying English.
2. Claire left her husband.
3. Glen is 40, and he just got married.
4. They canceled the English class.
5. All the students failed the exam.

CONVERSATION PAIR WORK

Express more regrets with your partner. Use the guide and the ideas from the box, or create a new conversation.

A: I should have ______ .
B: Why do you think that?
A: Well, I might have ______ .
B: Could be. But you never know. You might ______ …

Continue the conversation in your <u>own</u> way.

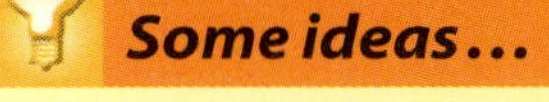

Some ideas…

- taken a job [at Microsoft]
- bought a [sports car]
- studied [medicine]
- married [Pat]
- your own idea: ____________

LESSON

Discuss Skills, Abilities, and Qualifications

A **VOCABULARY. Skills and abilities. Listen and practice.**

talents abilities in art, music, mathematics, etc. that you are born with
She was born with talents in both mathematics and art.

skills abilities that you learn, such as cooking, speaking a foreign language, or driving
She has several publishing skills: writing, editing, and illustrating.

experience time spent working at a job in the past
Sally has a lot of experience in sales. She has worked at three companies.

knowledge understanding of or familiarity with a subject, gained from experience or study
Anna has extensive knowledge of the history of film. You can ask her which classics to see.

B **LISTENING COMPREHENSION. Listen to nine people being interviewed at an international job fair. Stop after each interview and match each interviewee with his or her qualification.**

Interviewee	Qualification
h 1. Sonia Espinoza	a. a good memory
___ 2. Silvano Lucastro	b. artistic ability
___ 3. Ivan Martinovic	c. mathematical ability
___ 4. Agnes Lukins	d. logical thinking
___ 5. Elena Burgess	e. compassion
___ 6. Karen Trent	f. manual dexterity
___ 7. Ed Snodgrass	g. common sense
___ 8. Akiko Uzawa	h. athletic ability
___ 9. Mia Kim	i. leadership skills

C **PAIR WORK. With your partner, classify each qualification from exercise B. Do you agree on all the classifications? Discuss your opinions.**

A talent	A skill
artistic ability	

"I think artistic ability is a talent. You're born with it."

"I disagree. I think if you study art, you can develop artistic ability. I think it's a skill."

STEP 1. **Take the skills inventory.**

Careers, Jobs, Advanced Studies AND YOU

Whether you're looking for a job or interviewing for a school, interviewers expect you to answer questions about your interests, talents, skills, and experience. Take this inventory to prepare yourself for those questions.

Interests

Check the fields that interest you:

- ☐ business
- ☐ science
- ☐ education
- ☐ art
- ☐ manufacturing
- ☐ other _______

Qualifications

Check the qualifications you believe you have:

- ☐ manual dexterity
- ☐ logical thinking
- ☐ mathematical ability
- ☐ common sense
- ☐ athletic ability
- ☐ artistic ability
- ☐ compassion
- ☐ a good memory
- ☐ leadership skills
- ☐ other _______

Experience

Briefly note information about your experience, skills, and any special knowledge you have.

Experience: ______________________________

Skills: ______________________________

Special knowledge: ______________________________

Qualification	Example
mathematical ability	I love number puzzles. I'm great at them!

STEP 2. **On the notepad, write specific examples of your qualifications.**

Qualification	Example

STEP 3. **ROLE PLAY.** **Role-play an interview for a job, for career advice, or for entry into a school. Talk about interests, qualifications, skills, and experience.**

NEED HELP? **Here's language you already know:**

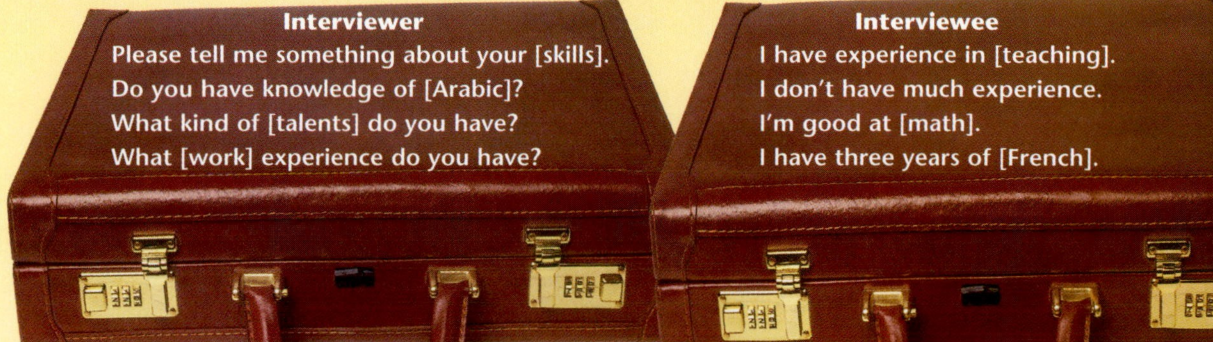

Interviewer
Please tell me something about your [skills].
Do you have knowledge of [Arabic]?
What kind of [talents] do you have?
What [work] experience do you have?
Interviewee
I have experience in [teaching].
I don't have much experience.
I'm good at [math].
I have three years of [French].

Discuss Work and Life Decisions

LESSON

 **READING WARM-UP.** **Can you name some great humanitarians—people who have made or who are making an important difference in the world?**

 **READING.** **Read about the lifework of two humanitarians. Why do you think these people are internationally known?**

PEOPLE WHO CHANGED THE WORLD

Mahatma Gandhi

"Non-violence is not a weapon of the weak. It is a weapon of the strongest and the bravest." —Mahatma Gandhi

Mohandas Karamchand Gandhi believed that the way people behave is more important than what they accomplish. Gandhi studied law but became known for social action. He practiced non-violence to help India achieve independence from Britain.

In 1947, India was granted independence, but the country was broken into two states—India and Pakistan—and fighting between Hindus and Muslims began. But Gandhi believed in an India where Hindus and Muslims could live together in peace. On January 13, 1948, at the age of 78, Gandhi began a fast, not eating anything for days, with the purpose of stopping the war. After five days, the opposing leaders said they would stop the fighting and Gandhi broke his fast and started eating again.

Sadly, twelve days later Gandhi was assassinated by a Hindu fanatic who strongly opposed his vision of an India for both Hindus and Muslims. The Indian people called Gandhi "Mahatma," meaning "Great Soul."

Mahatma Gandhi
Indian Spiritual / Political Leader and Humanitarian 1869–1948

Albert Schweitzer

"Man must cease attributing his problems to his environment, and learn again to exercise his will—his personal responsibility." —Albert Schweitzer

Albert Schweitzer was born in Alsace, Germany, which is now a part of France. By the time he was 21, Schweitzer had decided on the course for his life. For nine years he would dedicate himself to the study of science, music, and religion. Then he would devote the rest of his life to serving humanity directly. Before he was 30, he was a respected writer, an organist, and an expert on the life and work of Johann Sebastian Bach.

Albert Schweitzer
German Philosopher, Physician, and Humanitarian 1875–1965

In 1904, Schweitzer was inspired to help sick people in the world, so he studied medicine at the University of Strasbourg. He founded a hospital in French Equatorial Africa in 1913. Over the years, he built a large hospital that served thousands of Africans. In 1952, Schweitzer received the Nobel Prize for Peace. He used his $33,000 Nobel Prize to expand the hospital and to build a place to take care of people who had the terrible disease of leprosy.

Schweitzer based his personal philosophy on a love and respect for life and on a deep commitment to serve humanity through thought and action.

SOURCE: Adapted from www.lucidcafe.com

C PAIR WORK. Use <u>must have</u>, <u>might have</u>, <u>may have</u>, and <u>could have</u> to discuss the following questions.

1. Why do you think Schweitzer and Gandhi spent their lives helping other people?
2. Instead of being humanitarians, what might Gandhi and Schweitzer have been? What could they have done with their lives?

D DISCUSSION. In what ways are Mahatma Gandhi and Albert Schweitzer humanitarians? Do you admire how they chose to live their lives? Do you know any other humanitarians? What did they do?

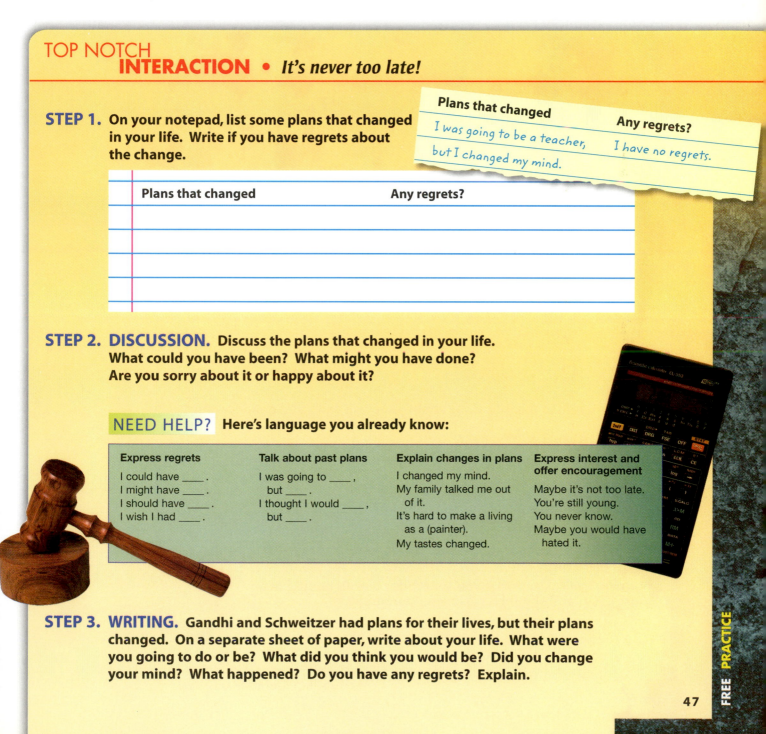

TOP NOTCH INTERACTION • *It's never too late!*

STEP 1. On your notepad, list some plans that changed in your life. Write if you have regrets about the change.

Plans that changed	Any regrets?
I was going to be a teacher, but I changed my mind.	I have no regrets.

Plans that changed	Any regrets?

STEP 2. DISCUSSION. Discuss the plans that changed in your life. What could you have been? What might you have done? Are you sorry about it or happy about it?

NEED HELP? Here's language you already know:

Express regrets	Talk about past plans	Explain changes in plans	Express interest and offer encouragement
I could have ____. I might have ____. I should have ____. I wish I had ____.	I was going to ____, but ____. I thought I would ____, but ____.	I changed my mind. My family talked me out of it. It's hard to make a living as a (painter). My tastes changed.	Maybe it's not too late. You're still young. You never know. Maybe you would have hated it.

STEP 3. WRITING. Gandhi and Schweitzer had plans for their lives, but their plans changed. On a separate sheet of paper, write about your life. What were you going to do or be? What did you think you would be? Did you change your mind? What happened? Do you have any regrets? Explain.

UNIT 4 CHECKPOINT

A **LISTENING COMPREHENSION.** **Listen to the conversations. Complete the chart.**

	Why did the person change his / her mind?	Any regrets?
1.		yes / no
2.		yes / no
3.		yes / no
4.		yes / no

B **Complete each statement of belief about the future, using would.**

1. When I was a child, I thought I ____________________.
2. My parents believed ____________________.
3. My teachers were sure ____________________.
4. When I finished school, I didn't know ____________________.

C **Explain the meaning of each of the following qualifications. Then write an occupation or course of study for a person with each qualification.**

Qualification	Definition	Occupation or Study
1. athletic ability		
2. artistic ability		
3. mathematical ability		
4. logical thinking ability		
5. a good memory		
6. leadership skills		

D **Write answers to the questions about your own skills and qualifications.**

1. What talents do you have? ____________________
2. What work experience do you have? ____________________
3. What skills do you have? ____________________
4. What special knowledge do you have? ____________________

E **WRITING.** **On a separate sheet of paper, write a paragraph about Mahatma Gandhi, Albert Schweitzer, or another great humanitarian. Use was going to, would, may or might have, must have, and should have in your paragraph.**

***TOP NOTCH* PROJECT**
Write advertisements for jobs. Include requirements for experience and skills.

***TOP NOTCH* WEBSITE**
For Unit 4 online activities, visit the *Top Notch* Companion Website at www.longman.com/topnotch.

Unit Wrap-Up

- **Narration.** Tell the life story of the Wileys. Talk about the expectations their parents had, their own expectations, and what happened.

Michael | **Carlota**

Their parents' plans and dreams for them

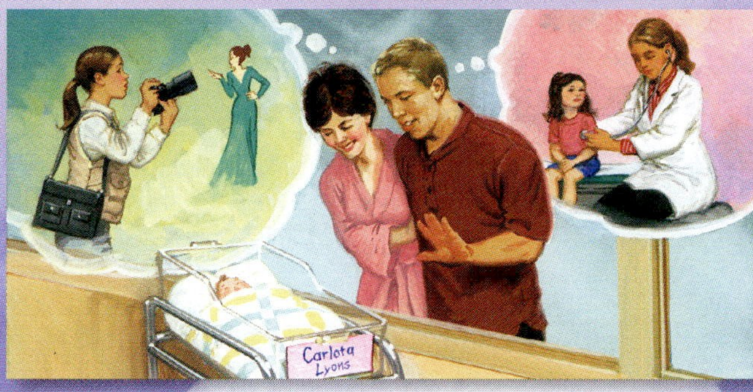

1990

Their wishes and dreams for themselves

Now

Their actual choices and regrets

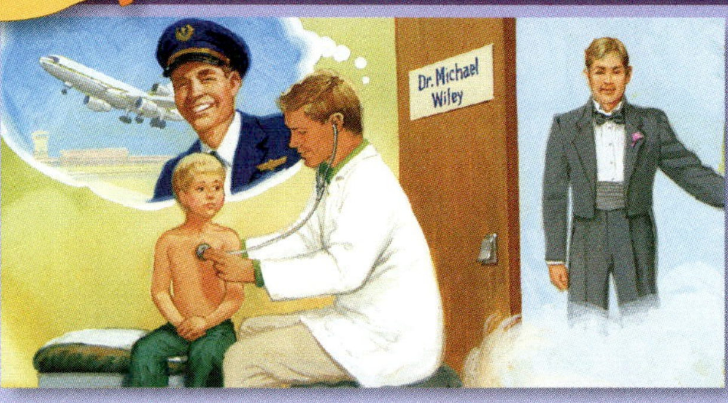

Now I can ...

- ☐ explain a change in life and work choices.
- ☐ express regrets about decisions.
- ☐ discuss skills, abilities, and qualifications.
- ☐ discuss work and life decisions.

UNIT 5

Holidays and Traditions

UNIT GOALS

1 Find out about a holiday
2 Ask about the customs of another culture
3 Describe a holiday or celebration
4 Explain wedding traditions

A TOPIC PREVIEW. Look at the pictures. Which traditions are you familiar with? Which ones would you like to know more about?

▲ A mariachi band in the State of Jalisco, Mexico, where mariachi was born

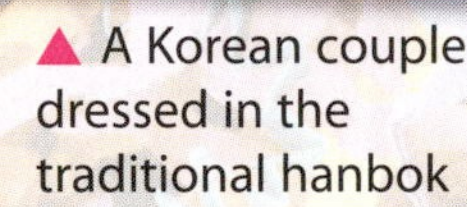

▲ A Korean couple dressed in the traditional hanbok

▲ Thanksgiving in the United States, featuring turkey, the traditional Thanksgiving food

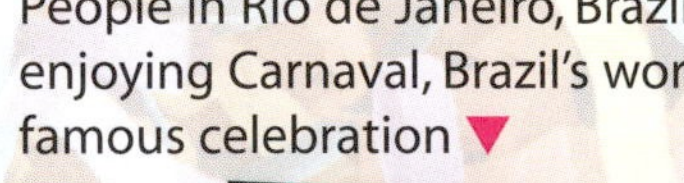

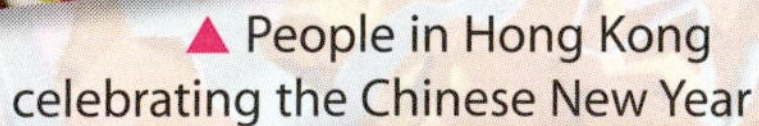

▲ People in Hong Kong celebrating the Chinese New Year

People in Rio de Janeiro, Brazil, enjoying Carnaval, Brazil's world-famous celebration ▼

Egyptians buying traditional sweets for the feast of Eid ul-Fitr at the end of Ramadan, the most important observance in Islam ▼

B DISCUSSION. Why do people think it is important to keep traditions alive? Do you think it is important to learn about the customs and traditions of other religions and cultures?

C **SOUND BITES.** **Read along silently as you listen to a conversation during a coffee break at an international meeting.**

MAYA: Wow! That dress Su-min is wearing is spectacular. What was the occasion?
MIN-JIN: Chuseok. The dress is called a hanbok.
MAYA: Did you say "Chuseok"? What's that—a holiday?
MIN-JIN: That's right. It's a Korean harvest celebration. It takes place in September or October each year.
MAYA: Oh yeah? What does everybody do?
MIN-JIN: We get together with our relatives. The airports and train stations are mobbed with passengers, and the roads are impossible. It takes hours to get anywhere.
MAYA: Every country's got at least one holiday like that!

IN OTHER WORDS. **Say each statement in another way.**

1. That dress is spectacular.
2. It takes place in September.
3. We get together with our relatives.
4. The train stations are mobbed with passengers.
5. The roads are impossible.

On a separate sheet of paper, write five sentences about holidays in your country. Use the following words or phrases: spectacular, take place, get together with, mobbed with people, and impossible.

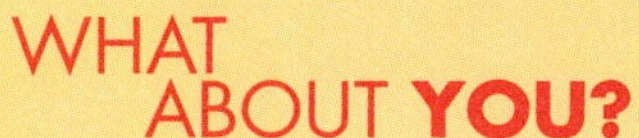

Complete the chart. Give examples and information about holiday traditions in your country.

a clothing item:	When is it worn?
a type of music:	When is it played?
a food:	When is it eaten?
a dance:	When is it danced?
a special event:	What happens?

LESSON

1 Find out about a Holiday

CONVERSATION MODEL Read and listen.

A: I heard there's going to be a holiday.
B: That's right. The Harvest Moon Festival.
A: What kind of holiday is that?
B: It's a seasonal holiday that takes place in autumn. People spend time with their families and eat moon cakes.
A: Well, have a great Harvest Moon Festival!
B: Thanks! Same to you!

Rhythm and intonation practice

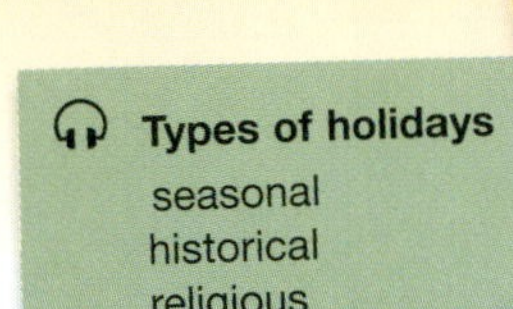

Types of holidays
seasonal
historical
religious

a moon cake

A VOCABULARY. Ways to commemorate a holiday. Listen and practice.

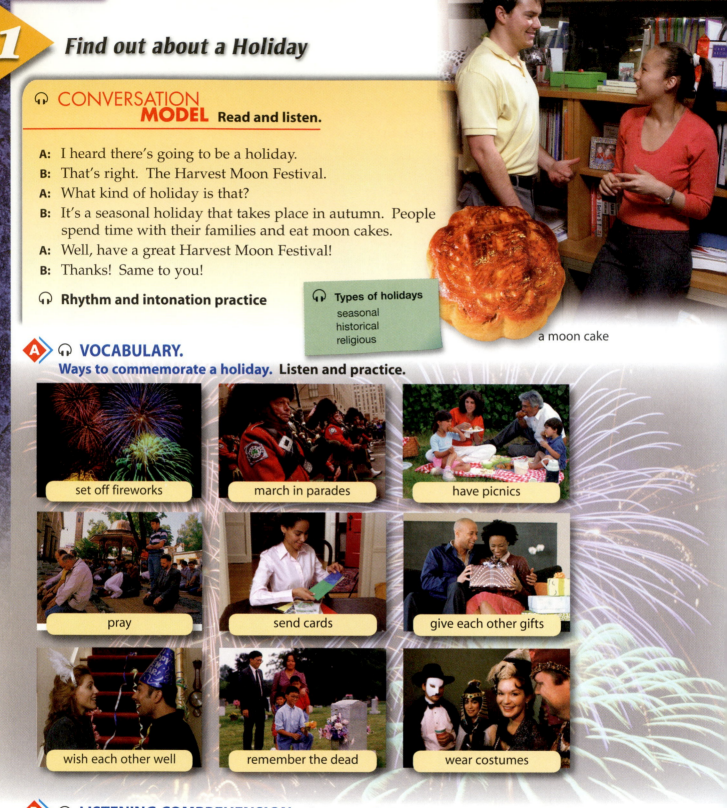

set off fireworks

march in parades

have picnics

pray

send cards

give each other gifts

wish each other well

remember the dead

wear costumes

B LISTENING COMPREHENSION. Listen carefully to the descriptions of holidays. Write the type of holiday and what people do to celebrate.

	Type of holiday	What people do to celebrate
Mardi Gras (U.S.)		
Bastille Day (France)		
Tsagaan Sar (Mongolia)		

GRAMMAR. Adjective clauses with subject relative pronouns

Use an adjective clause to identify or give information about a noun or an indefinite pronoun such as someone, something, etc. Begin an adjective clause with the relative pronouns who or that for adjective clauses that describe people. Use that for adjective clauses that describe things.

A mariachi singer is someone **who** (or **that**) **sings traditional Mexican music**.
Carnaval is a great holiday for people **who** (or **that**) **like parades**.
Anyone **who** (or **that**) **doesn't wear a costume** can't go to the festival.
Halloween is a celebration **that takes place in October**.
The parade **that takes place on Bastille Day** is very exciting.

BE CAREFUL! Don't use a subject pronoun after the relative pronoun.
Don't say: Halloween is a celebration that ~~it~~ takes place in October.

PAGES G7–G9
For more …

Underline the adjective clauses and circle the relative pronouns. Then draw an arrow from the relative pronoun to the noun or pronoun that it describes.

1. Ramadan is a religious tradition that is observed by Muslims all over the world.
2. Chuseok is a Korean holiday that celebrates the yearly harvest.
3. The gifts that people usually give to each other are not very expensive.
4. In the United States, a person who is invited for dinner often brings a gift to eat or drink.
5. The Day of the Dead in Mexico is a celebration that takes place in November.
6. The celebrations that take place in Brazil during Carnaval are a lot of fun.

E PAIR WORK. Create five sentences with adjective clauses to describe some holidays in your country. Use the models to begin.

… is a (religious) holiday that …

… is a great holiday for people who …

CONVERSATION PAIR WORK

Role-play a conversation with a visitor to your country. Exchange information about holidays. Start like this, or create a new conversation.

A: I heard there's going to be a holiday next _____.
B: That's right. _____.
A: What kind of holiday is that?
B: _____ …

Continue the conversation in your own way.

Ways to give good wishes on holidays
Have a nice / good / great [Carnaval]!
Have a happy [New Year]!
Enjoy yourself on [Chuseok]!

LESSON

2 Ask about the Customs of Another Culture

CONVERSATION MODEL Read and listen.

A: Do you mind if I ask you something?
B: Of course not. What's up?
A: I'm not sure of the customs here. When you're invited for dinner, should you bring the host a gift?
B: Yes. That's a good idea. But the gift that you bring should be small.
A: Would flowers be appropriate?
B: Absolutely perfect!
A: Thanks. It's a good thing I asked.

Rhythm and intonation practice

A GRAMMAR. Adjective clauses with object relative pronouns

In some adjective clauses, the relative pronoun is the subject of the clause.

The person **who comes for dinner** should bring a gift.
[who = subject because he or she is the performer of the action]

In other adjective clauses, the relative pronoun is the object of the clause.

The person **who** [or **whom**] **you invite** should bring a gift.
[who (or whom) = object because he or she is the receiver of the action]

When the relative pronoun is the object of the clause, it may be omitted.

The book **that you bought** gives great information about holidays. OR
The book **you bought** gives great information about holidays.

When the relative pronoun is the subject of the clause, it may NOT be omitted.

The author **who wrote that book** did a great job.
NOT ~~The author wrote that book did a great job~~.

PAGE G9
For more ...

B PRONUNCIATION. "Thought groups." Notice how rhythm indicates how thoughts are grouped. Listen and repeat.

1. The person who comes for dinner should bring flowers.
2. The man we invited to the party is from Senegal.
3. The song that you were listening to is fado music from Portugal.
4. The Cherry Blossom Festival is a holiday that is celebrated in Japan every spring.

maracas, traditional musical instruments of the Caribbean and Latin America

 **PAIR WORK. Discuss whether the relative pronoun can be deleted. If it can be deleted, cross it out.**

1. The traditional Chinese dress ~~that~~ she has is called a cheongsam.
2. The man who you were talking with plays in a mariachi band.
3. Anzac Day is a holiday that people in Australia and New Zealand celebrate to remember the soldiers who died in wars.
4. People who visit other countries should find out about the local customs.
5. The young people whom you saw in the parade today were all wearing traditional costumes.

A bouquet of flowers is a popular gift in many countries.

 **Correct the error in each sentence.**

1. Putting butter on a child's nose is a birthday tradition that ~~it~~ is celebrated on the Atlantic coast of Canada.
2. On the Day of the Dead, Mexicans remember family members who they have died.
3. The older couple we saw at the restaurant they were doing the tango.
4. La Tomatina is a festival that it is celebrated in Bunol, Spain.
5. The singer performed at Casey Hall last night is well known all over Europe.

CONVERSATION PAIR WORK

Role-play a conversation with a visitor to your country. Discuss customs. Use the guide and the ideas from the box, or create a new conversation.

A: Do you mind if I ask you something?
B: Of course not. What's up?
A: I'm not sure about the customs here. When _____?
B: _____ …

Continue the conversation your own way.

 ***Some ideas…***

- **someone invites you out for dinner**
- **someone invites you to a party**
- **someone gives you a gift**
- **someone makes a special effort to help you**

LESSON

3 Describe a Holiday or Celebration

READING WARM-UP. What are your favorite holiday traditions?

READING. Read about some holiday traditions and observances from around the world. Are any of them familiar to you?

HOLIDAYS AROUND THE WORLD

Thailand's Wet Water Festival

Songkran marks the start of the Buddhist New Year in Thailand. It is a wild and wonderful festival in which people of all ages have fun dousing each other with water for three solid days. If you decide to stay indoors, you'll miss out on a great time!

Songkran began nearly a thousand years ago to celebrate the beginning of the farming season. It is a time when Thai people routinely do a thorough cleaning of their homes. Additionally, people make offerings to local temples and provide food and new robes for monks.

During Songkran there is singing and dancing in the streets, and lots of water. Visitors should expect to become totally drenched—and love every minute of it! On every side street, you'll find children waiting to throw water at you. Bus riders also need to be careful. Some people have been known to hurl buckets of water through open windows!

People douse each other with water during Songkran.

Ramadan, the Month of Fasting

"May you be well throughout the year," is the typical greeting during Ramadan, the ninth month of the Islamic calendar, a special month of the year for over one billion Muslims throughout the world. According to Islamic tradition, Ramadan marks the time when Muhammad received the word of God through the Koran. Throughout the month, Muslims fast—totally abstaining from food and drinks from the break of dawn until the setting of the sun. The usual practice is to have a pre-fast meal before dawn and a post-fast meal after sunset. It is also a time of increased worship and giving to the poor and the community. Ramadan ends with the festival of Eid ul-Fitr—three days of family celebrations—and eating!

Simon Bolivar's Birthday

Simon Bolivar was born on July 24, 1783 in Caracas, Venezuela. He is known throughout Latin America as "The Liberator" because of his fight for independence from Spain. He led the armies that freed Venezuela, Bolivia, Colombia, Ecuador, Peru, and Panama. He is memorialized in many ways, but two countries celebrate his birthday every July 24th—Venezuela and Ecuador. On that day, schools and most general businesses are closed and there are military parades and government ceremonies. But the malls are open and people usually use the holiday to go shopping.

Worshippers pray during Ramadan.

Bolivar led the fight for independence from Spain.

SOURCES: www.muhajabah.com and www.colostate.edu

C DISCUSSION.

1. How would you categorize each of the holidays in the article—religious, seasonal, or historic?
2. Which holiday or tradition do you find the most interesting? Why?
3. Do you know any holidays, observances, or traditions that are similar to these? What are they? How are they similar and different?

TOP NOTCH INTERACTION • *Do you mind if I ask you something?*

STEP 1. PAIR WORK. **Choose three holidays in your country. Discuss them and write some notes about them on your notepad.**

A historic holiday	A religious holiday	A seasonal holiday
name of holiday:	name of holiday:	name of holiday:
typical foods:	typical foods:	typical foods:
typical clothing:	typical clothing:	typical clothing:
other traditions:	other traditions:	other traditions:

STEP 2. ROLE PLAY. **Take turns with a different partner. One of you is a visitor to your country. Ask about and explain your holidays and traditions. Use your notepad for ideas.**

NEED HELP? **Here's language you already know:**

Visitor
Do you mind if I ask you ____?
I hear people ____.
Is it possible to ____?
What do people do?
I'm not sure of the customs here.
Would ____ be appropriate?
It's a good thing I asked!
It's a ____, isn't it?

Resident
It's a great day for ____.
It's customary to ____.
It's offensive to ____.
____ is taboo.
It's impolite to ____.
It's probably best to ____.
That must be ____.
You can eat ____.
You can wear ____.

traditional Japanese origami

Explain Wedding Traditions

LESSON

A **VOCABULARY. Getting married. Listen and practice.**

an engagement an agreement to marry someone

get engaged agree to marry

a ceremony a formal set of actions used at an important social or religious event such as a wedding

a wedding a marriage ceremony, especially one with a religious service

a reception a large formal party after a ceremony

a honeymoon a vacation taken by two newlyweds

The wedding couple

a bride a woman at the time she gets married

a groom a man at the time he gets married

newlyweds the bride and groom after the wedding

B **Read about some wedding traditions in many English-speaking countries. Then use the vocabulary to describe a wedding tradition you are familiar with.**

The bride throws her bouquet after **the wedding ceremony**. The woman who catches the bouquet is believed to be the next to get married.

The newlyweds cut the cake together **at the wedding reception**.

The groom carries the bride "across the threshold," through the doorway into their new home. Soon after the wedding, they **go on their honeymoon**.

C **LISTENING COMPREHENSION. Listen carefully to Part 1 of a lecture about a traditional wedding in India. Then read the statements and listen again. Check the statements that are true. Correct the statements that are false.**

PART 1. Before the wedding

☐ **1.** A traditional Hindu wedding celebration can last for more than five days.
☐ **2.** The wedding date is chosen based on the date the bride prefers.
☐ **3.** Musicians visit the bride's home and play traditional music.
☐ **4.** The groom's relatives wash the groom with coconut or olive oil.
☐ **5.** An older person in the family offers the groom food.
☐ **6.** The bride's relatives paint her face, arms, hands, and feet.

Now listen carefully to Part 2 of the lecture. Then read the statements and listen again. Check the statements that are true. Correct the statements that are false.

PART 2. On the day of the wedding

- ☐ **7.** Relatives wash the bride's and groom's hands.
- ☐ **8.** The bride is seated behind a cloth so the groom cannot see her.
- ☐ **9.** Relatives throw rice grains at the bride and groom.
- ☐ **10.** The couple gives each other rings made of flowers and some rice.
- ☐ **11.** The groom places a flower necklace over the bride's neck.

D DISCUSSION. Are any of the traditions described in the listening similar to those in your country? Which traditions sounded the most interesting to you? Why?

TOP NOTCH INTERACTION • *Something old and something new*

STEP 1. PAIR WORK. Read the sayings and proverbs about weddings and marriage. Explain what you think each one means. Do you find any of them offensive? What sayings or proverbs about weddings do you know in your own language?

Marry off your son when you wish. Marry off your daughter when you can.
Italy

Marriages are all happy. It's having breakfast together that causes all the trouble.
Ireland

Marriage is just friendship if there are no children.
South Africa

The woman cries before the wedding and the man after.
Poland

A bride should wear something old and something new, something borrowed, and something blue.
the U.K.

STEP 2. GROUP WORK. On your notepad, make a list of traditions for weddings in your country. Compare your lists with those of other groups.

before a wedding:

at a wedding ceremony:

after a wedding:

STEP 3. WRITING. Write a paragraph describing the wedding traditions in your country.

FREE PRACTICE

UNIT 5 CHECKPOINT

A **LISTENING COMPREHENSION.** **Listen to each conversation and check the occasion or people they are talking about.**

1. ☐ the engagement ☐ the reception ☐ the honeymoon
2. ☐ the engagement ☐ the reception ☐ the honeymoon
3. ☐ the bride ☐ the groom ☐ the relatives
4. ☐ the bride ☐ the groom ☐ the relatives

B **Answer each question in your own way.**

1. What's the most important holiday in your country? What kind of a holiday is it (seasonal, historical, religious)?
   YOU ______________________________
2. What's the longest holiday in your country? How long is it?
   YOU ______________________________
3. What's the most interesting wedding tradition in your country?
   YOU ______________________________

TOP NOTCH **SONG**
"Endless Holiday"
Lyrics on last book page.

TOP NOTCH **PROJECT**
Use the library or the Internet to research a holiday or wedding customs from another country. Tell your classmates about it.

TOP NOTCH **WEBSITE**
For Unit 5 online activities, visit the *Top Notch* Companion Website at www.longman.com/topnotch.

C **Complete each statement. Then write the name of a holiday or celebration for each one.**

	Holiday or celebration
1. Name a holiday when people ______ fireworks.	______
2. Name a holiday when people ______ in parades.	______
3. Name a holiday when people ______ picnics.	______
4. Name a holiday when people ______ time with their families.	______
5. Name a holiday when people ______ costumes.	______
6. Name a holiday when people give ______ gifts.	______
7. Name a holiday when people wish ______ well.	______

D **Complete each sentence with an adjective clause.**

1. A groom is a man *who has just gotten married*.
2. Ramadan is a religious observance ______________________________.
3. A honeymoon is a vacation ______________________________.
4. A hanbok is a traditional dress ______________________________.
5. Songkran is a holiday ______________________________.
6. Simon Bolivar was a Venezuelan ______________________________.

E **WRITING.** **Describe a holiday or a tradition in your country. When does it take place? What do people do? What are the origins of these customs / traditions?**

UNIT WRAP-UP

- **Vocabulary.** Name the ways people are celebrating the holiday.
- **Social language.** Create a conversation for the man and woman.
- **Grammar.** Describe what is happening on this holiday, using adjective clauses. *There are people who are wearing costumes in the parade.*

Now I can ...

- ☐ find out about a holiday.
- ☐ ask about the customs of another culture.
- ☐ describe a holiday or celebration.
- ☐ explain wedding traditions.

UNIT 6

Disasters and Emergencies

UNIT GOALS

1 Convey a message
2 Report news
3 Prepare for an emergency
4 Describe natural disasters

TOPIC PREVIEW. Look at three historic news events. Which of these famous disasters are you familiar with?

"All the News That's Fit to Print."

The New York Times.

TITANIC SINKS FOUR HOURS AFTER HITTING ICEBERG; 866 RESCUED BY CARPATHIA, PROBABLY 1250 PERISH; ISMAY SAFE, MRS. ASTOR MAYBE, NOTED NAMES MISSING

Col. Astor and Bride, Isidor Straus and Wife, and Maj. Butt Aboard.

"RULE OF SEA" FOLLOWED

Women and Children Put Over in Lifeboats and Are Supposed to be Safe on Carpathia.

PICKED UP AFTER 8 HOURS

Vincent Astor Calls at White Star Office for News of His Father and Leaves Weeping.

FRANKLIN HOPEFUL ALL DAY

Manager of the Line Insisted Titanic Was Unsinkable Even After She Had Gone Down.

HEAD OF THE LINE ABOARD

Biggest Liner Plunges to the Bottom at 2:20 A.M.

RESCUERS THERE TOO LATE

Except to Pick Up the Few Hundreds Who Took to the Lifeboats.

WOMEN AND CHILDREN FIRST

Cunarder Carpathia Rushing to New York with the Survivors.

SEA SEARCH FOR OTHERS

The California Stands By on Chance of Picking Up Other Boats or Rafts.

OLYMPIC SENDS THE NEWS

The Lost Titanic Being Towed Out of Belfast Harbor.

PARTIAL LIST OF THE SAVED.

...TIVITY YESTERDAY AS THE APEX OF THE FIGHT AGAINST INFLUENZA WAS ...

OPEN AIR AND VACCINE WILL FIGHT DISEASE

300,000 Cases in State Are Feared Unless Patients Kept in Uncovered Hospitals

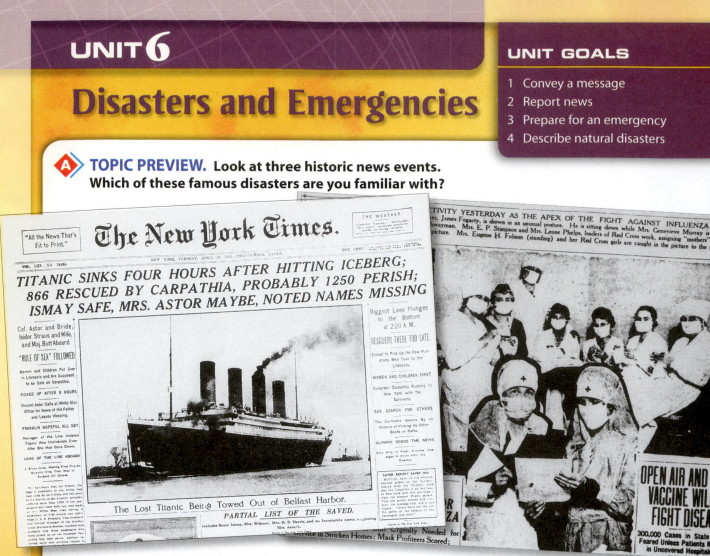

On April 10, 1912, the British ocean liner Titanic sinks with a loss of over 1,500 people.

The influenza epidemic of 1918-19 leaves an estimated 25 million people dead worldwide.

Quake triggers walls of water

Killer waves hit Southeast Asia

PHUKET, Thailand—The killer tidal waves struck with terrifying speed, obliterating entire villages and sweeping away tourists, boats, cars and buildings.

Witnesses described vast 10-meter (33-feet) walls of water careering at speed into the coastline of Indonesia, Thailand, Malaysia, Sri Lanka, India, Bangladesh and the Maldives on Sunday.

The many foreigners enjoying the Christmas holiday on Thailand's western coast were left stunned by the tsunamis, which were caused by a huge earthquake off northern Indonesia.

"Just out of nowhere, suddenly the streets are awash and people just running and screaming from the beach," said Australian politician John Hyde, who was in southern Thailand when the tsunami hit.

"All the windows are blown in, [there's] debris everywhere," Hyde told the Australian Broadcasting Corp.

Australian tourist Raeshell Tang said she and her husband Mark saw a gigantic wave hit from their hotel room in Phuket, on Thailand's southwest coast.

"We just went out onto the balcony to see what the day was going to be like and there it was in front of us, the tidal wave," she said.

SEE QUAKE/A6

Quake, tidal waves kill thousands

Provisional death toll at 1100 GMT

COLOMBO, Sri Lanka—The most powerful earthquake in 40 years triggered massive tidal waves that slammed into coastlines across Asia Sunday, killing as many as 3,000 people in Sri Lanka, Indonesia, India, Malaysia, Maldives and Thailand.

Tourists, fishermen, homes and cars were swept away by walls of water unleashed by the 8.9-magnitude earthquake, centered off the west coast of the Indonesian island of Sumatra, where at least 94 people were killed by floods and collapsing buildings, officials said.

But the scope of the disaster became apparent only after waves as high as six meters (20 feet) crashed into coastal areas throughout the Indian Ocean and Adaman Sea.

In Sri Lanka—some 1,600 kilometers (1,000 miles) west of the epicenter—hospitals, police reported 1,000 dead and more than 500,000 affected by the wall of water.

Reports from India said as many as 500 had been killed along the southern coast. Another 61 were confirmed dead in Thai-

On December 26, 2004, a 9.0-magnitude earthquake created a tsunami that killed over 250,000 people in Indonesia, Sri Lanka, India, Thailand, and other countries.

DISCUSSION. Why do you think the news is often about disasters? What other kinds of news stories make headlines? What happens to the "good news"?

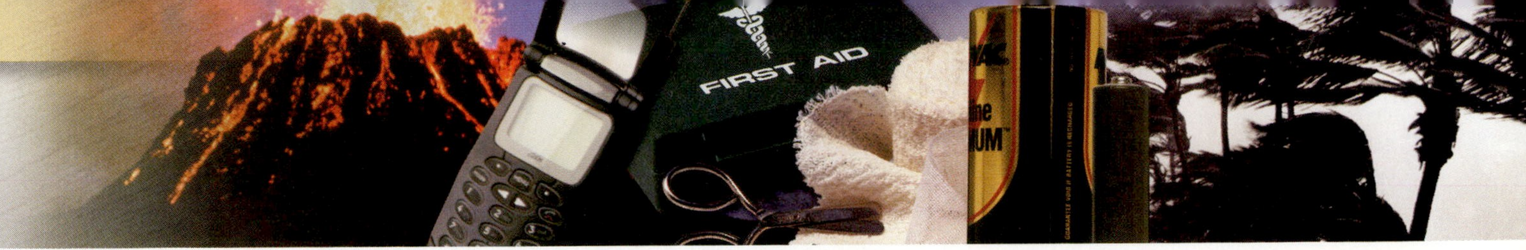

C SOUND BITES. Read along silently as you listen to a natural conversation.

RACHEL: Oh, my goodness! Look at this breaking news from Romania.
TOM: What happened?
RACHEL: It says there was a huge earthquake there yesterday. It was 8.6 on the Richter scale. What a disaster!
TOM: 8.6? That's gigantic! Any word on casualties?
RACHEL: They say there's a lot of property damage, but luckily it struck during the day. So far no reports of deaths or injuries.
TOM: Well, let's hope for the best.
RACHEL: I wonder if 8.6 is a record.
TOM: Believe it or not, no. There was once a 9.5 near Chile.

D UNDERSTANDING FROM CONTEXT. Find a word or expression in the conversation that means …

1. news that's happening right now.
2. any terrible event where many people are hurt or killed.
3. very, very large.
4. deaths and injuries.
5. the largest in history.
6. it's unbelievable but true.

WHAT ABOUT YOU?

Check the places you get the news. Then write the name of the newspaper, magazine, TV station, etc.

	Source	Name
☐	a daily newspaper	
☐	a weekly news magazine	
☐	TV	
☐	the radio	
☐	the Internet	
☐	word of mouth	

DISCUSSION. **Which news sources do you think are the best for breaking news? Weather forecasts? Emergency information? Explain your reasons and give examples.**

LESSON

Convey a Message

CONVERSATION MODEL Read and listen.

A: I'm on the line with your parents. Would you like to say hello?
B: I would, but I'm running late.
A: Anything you'd like me to tell them?
B: Yes. Please tell them to watch the news. There's a storm on its way.
A: Will do.

 **Rhythm and intonation practice**

A GRAMMAR. Indirect speech: imperatives

When you report what someone said, but without quoting the exact words, use indirect speech. Don't use quotation marks when you write indirect speech.

direct speech: Peter said, "Come for dinner on Sunday."
indirect speech: Peter said to come for dinner on Sunday.

In indirect speech, an imperative becomes an infinitive.

They said, "**Read** the weather forecast." They said **to read** the weather forecast.
She says, "**Don't go** without a full tank of gas." She says **not to go** without a full tank of gas.

Make changes in pronouns and time expressions in indirect speech to preserve the speaker's original meaning.

She told Dan, "Call **me tomorrow**." She told Dan to call **her the next day**.

PAGE G10
For more ...

B PAIR WORK. With a partner, say what you think the speaker's original words were.

1. He told them to call him at three. "(Please) call me at three."
2. The police said to leave a window or door open when there's going to be a severe storm.
3. She told his parents to read the emergency instructions in the newspaper.
4. They told her to get vaccinated before her trip to Tanzania.
5. She asked him to pick up some supplies for her on the way home.
6. They told me not to call them after nine.

C **Rewrite each statement in indirect speech, making necessary changes.**

1. Martha told me, "Be home before the storm."
   Martha told me to be home before the storm.
2. Everyone says, "Get ready for a big storm tomorrow."
   ______
3. The radio says, "Get supplies of food and water in case the roads are closed."
   ______
4. They told her, "Don't be home too late."
   ______
5. Maria always tells him, "Don't leave your doors open."
   ______

D **PRONUNCIATION. Direct and indirect speech: rhythm. Listen to the rhythm of sentences in direct and indirect speech. Then repeat.**

He said, [pause] "Be home before midnight."
He said to be home before midnight.

I told your parents, [pause] "Get a flu shot at the clinic."
I told your parents to get a flu shot at the clinic.

CONVERSATION PAIR WORK

Role-play conveying a message. Use the guide, the possible excuses, and the possible messages, or create a new conversation.

A: I'm on the line with ____. Would you like to say hello?
B: I would, but ____.
A: Anything you'd like me to tell ____?
B: Yes. Please ____.
A: ____.

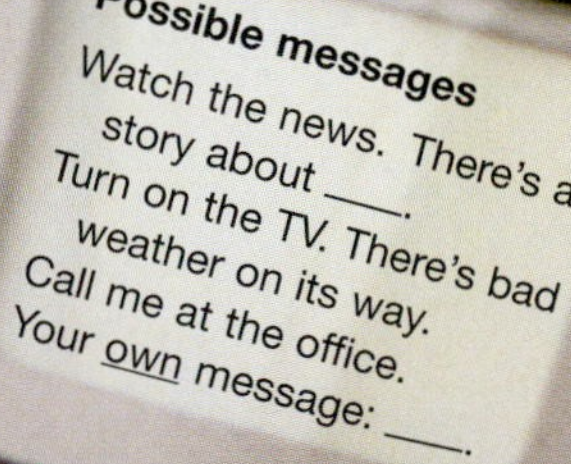

Possible messages
Watch the news. There's a story about ____.
Turn on the TV. There's bad weather on its way.
Call me at the office.
Your own message: ____.

Possible excuses
I'm running late.
I have an appointment.
I don't have time right now.

LESSON

2 Report News

CONVERSATION MODEL Read and listen.

A: What's going on in the news today?
B: Well, there was a terrible storm in the south.
A: Really?
B: Yes. It says lots of houses were destroyed.
A: What a shame.
B: But there were no deaths.
A: Thank goodness for that.

Rhythm and intonation practice

A GRAMMAR. Indirect speech: say and tell; tense changes

Use tell when you mention the listener(s). Use say when you don't.

Maggie **told her parents** to stay home. (listeners mentioned)
Maggie **said** to stay home. (listener not mentioned)

When say or tell are in the past tense, the verbs in the indirect speech statement often change. Present becomes past. Past becomes past perfect.

They **said**, "The weather **is** awful." They **said** (that) the weather **was** awful.
Dan **said**, "We all **had** the flu." Dan **said** (that) they **had** all **had** the flu.

PAGES G10–G11
For more ...

B Circle the correct verbs for indirect speech.

My Great-Grandmother Meets Hurricane Cleo

Hurricane Cleo struck the United States in August, 1964. My great-grandmother, Ana, was traveling in Miami when the hurricane struck. She (1. said / told) me that she still remembers how scared everyone was. She (2. said / told) me that one morning the hotel (3. calls / called) her room and (4. said / told) her that a big storm (5. is / was) on its way. They (6. said / told) that all hotel guests (7. have to / had to) stay in the hotel until the weather service (8. tell / said) that it (9. is / was) safe to leave. She stayed in her room and she didn't know what happened until the storm was over. When she turned on the TV, the reports (10. said / told) that a lot of people (11. have been / had been) injured and that all the roads (12. are / were) flooded. She always (13. says / said) that she still (14. feels / felt) lucky to have survived Hurricane Cleo.

C VOCABULARY. Severe weather events. Listen and practice.

a tornado

a hurricane / a typhoon / a monsoon

a flood

a landslide

a drought

D Change each statement from direct speech to indirect speech, changing the verb tense in the indirect speech statement.

1. The TV reporter said, "The landslide is one of the worst in history."
2. He also said, "It caused the destruction of half the houses in the town."
3. My sister called and said, "There is no electricity because of the hurricane."
4. The newspaper said, "There was a tornado in the central part of the country."
5. The paper said, "The drought of 1999 was the worst natural disaster of the century."

E LISTENING COMPREHENSION. Listen to the news. Write each weather event.

1. ______________________
2. ______________________
3. ______________________
4. ______________________

F PAIR WORK. Listen to each report again. After each report, tell your partner what the reporter said. Use indirect speech and make necessary changes.

"She said it hadn't rained in months."

CONVERSATION PAIR WORK

Report what it says in the news. Use the headlines here or use real headlines from your newspaper. Start like this:

A: What's going on in the news today?
B: Well, ______ …

Continue the conversation in your own way.

Morning Herald
20,000 killed in earthquake in Iran

DAR POST
People flee flooded river valley

National News
Drought causes severe famine
Thousands die of hunger

Mercury
Avian influenza epidemic causes record deaths in Indonesia
Doctors urge children and elderly to receive vaccinations

Village Times
Severe dust storm hits Kabul suburbs
Extreme damage to cars, buildings

LESSON 3

Prepare for an Emergency

 **VOCABULARY. Emergency preparations and supplies. Listen and practice.**

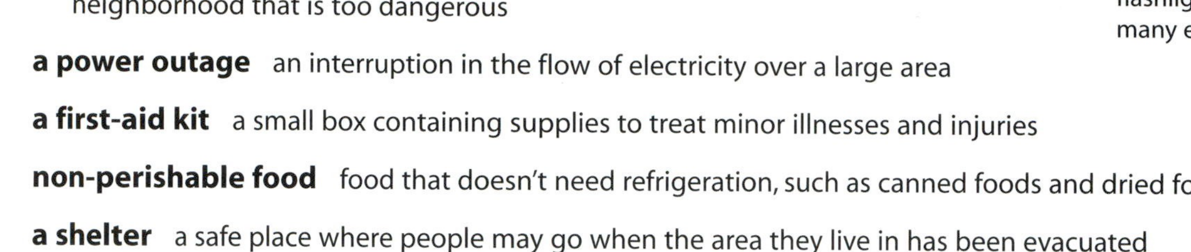

an emergency a very dangerous situation that requires immediate action

a flashlight a portable, battery-operated light

an evacuation the removal of all people from an area or neighborhood that is too dangerous

a power outage an interruption in the flow of electricity over a large area

a first-aid kit a small box containing supplies to treat minor illnesses and injuries

non-perishable food food that doesn't need refrigeration, such as canned foods and dried foods

a shelter a safe place where people may go when the area they live in has been evacuated

A battery-operated flashlight is a must in many emergencies.

 **LISTENING COMPREHENSION. Listen to an emergency radio broadcast. What's the emergency? Then listen again. Correct each of the following statements, using indirect speech.**

Example: He said you should stand near windows during the storm.

"No. He said not to stand near windows during the storm."

1. He said you should turn your refrigerator and freezer off.
2. He said that if there is a flood, you should put valuable papers on the lowest floor of your home.
3. He said you should read the newspapers for the location of shelters.

 **PAIR WORK. What did the radio announcer say in the emergency radio broadcast? Together, complete each statement in indirect speech. Listen again if necessary.**

1. According to the speaker, what should you do to get your car ready for evacuation?

   He said to ______________________.
2. What should you do with outdoor furniture?

   He said to ______________________.
3. What should you buy for flashlights and portable radios?

   He said to ______________________.
4. How should you get official instructions in case of an evacuation?

   He said to ______________________.
5. How should you prepare to have food and water, in case you have to stay indoors for several days?

   He said to ______________________.

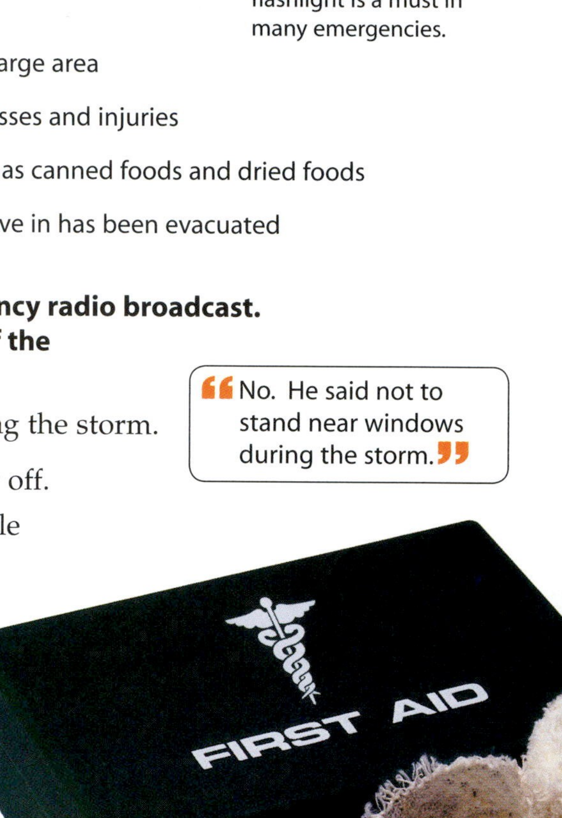

So is a first-aid kit with scissors and bandages.

TOP NOTCH INTERACTION • *Be prepared!*

STEP 1. GROUP WORK. **Divide into groups. Each group chooses an emergency to plan for. Then, write plans for your emergency on your notepads. Use the ideas to help you plan.**

Emergencies

a flood
a volcanic eruption
an earthquake
a tornado
a typhoon
other ________

Ideas to consider in your planning

- food, water, batteries, cell phones, and other supplies
- relatives that live in other places
- emergency telephone numbers
- family pets
- shelter

Emergency supplies	Goal	Reason
2 liters of water per person per day	have enough water	in case water is unsafe

Type of emergency:

Emergency supplies	Goal	Reason

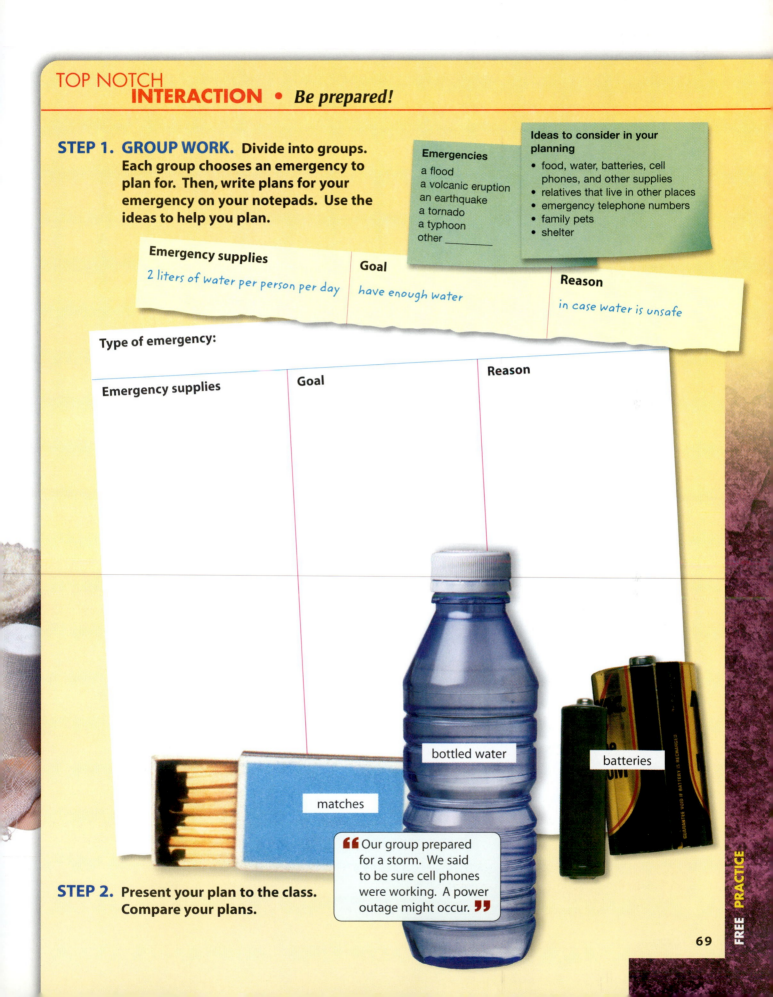

"Our group prepared for a storm. We said to be sure cell phones were working. A power outage might occur."

STEP 2. Present your plan to the class. Compare your plans.

FREE PRACTICE

LESSON

4 Describe Natural Disasters

A 🎧 **VOCABULARY. Discussing disasters. Listen and practice.**

natural disaster a disaster caused by nature, not people

death toll the number of people killed

destruction loss of buildings, roads, trees, and plants caused by disasters

casualties / victims people who are either injured or killed in a disaster

survivors people who are not killed when a disaster occurs

missing people who can't be found after a disaster

homeless people who have no place to live after a disaster

🎧 **Adjectives for describing disasters**

mild	!
moderate	!!
severe	!!!
deadly	!!!!
catastrophic	!!!!!

B **Have you or someone you know experienced a natural disaster? What happened? Use the vocabulary.**

C 🎧 **READING. Read about earthquakes. Why are earthquakes so frightening?**

Earthquakes

Damage to road in 1995 earthquake in Kobe, Japan

Earthquakes are among the deadliest natural disasters, causing the largest number of casualties, the highest death tolls, and the greatest destruction. In 1556 in China, the deadliest earthquake in history killed 830,000 people. But many other earthquakes have caused the deaths of more than 100,000 people, and it is not unusual, even in modern times, for an earthquake death toll to reach 20,000 to 30,000 people with hundreds of thousands left homeless.

There are four factors that affect the casualty rate and economic impact of earthquakes: magnitude, location, quality of construction of buildings, and timing.

Magnitude

The magnitude, or strength, of an earthquake is measured on the Richter scale, ranging from 1 to 10, with 10 being the greatest. Earthquakes over 6 on the Richter scale are often deadly, and those over 8 are generally catastrophic, causing terrible damage.

Location

However, a severe earthquake that is located far from population centers does not cause the same damage as a less severe one that occurs in the middle of a city. As an example, in 1960, the strongest earthquake ever recorded, 9.5 magnitude on the Richter scale, struck in the Pacific Ocean near the Chilean coastline, killing over 2,000 people and injuring another 3,000. If this quake had struck a city, it would have been catastrophic, and hundreds of thousands might have been killed. Similarly, in Alaska, in 1964, a magnitude 9.2 quake hit an area with few people, and the death toll was 117.

Quality of Construction

Furthermore, modern building construction techniques can lessen the death toll and economic impact of a moderate earthquake that would otherwise cause severe destruction of older-style buildings. In 2003, a terrible earthquake in the historic city of Bam in Iran caused the destruction of over 90% of the buildings, mostly due to old construction.

Timing

Finally, the time of occurrence of an earthquake can affect the number of deaths and casualties. Earthquakes that occur in the night, when people are indoors, usually cause a greater death toll than ones that occur when people are outdoors.

SOURCE: www.worldbookonline.com

Answer the questions, according to the information in the article.

“The article said the earthquake in 1556 in China was the deadliest in history.”

1. Which earthquake was the deadliest in history?
2. Which earthquake had the highest recorded Richter scale reading?
3. How can location affect the death toll of an earthquake?
4. How can building techniques lessen the destruction and economic impact of an earthquake?

DISCUSSION. How do magnitude and timing affect the casualty rate and economic impact of earthquakes?

TOP NOTCH INTERACTION • *What a disaster!*

STEP 1. PAIR WORK. Prepare a news report about fictional disasters and present it to your partner.

Partner A
from Star News Agency
Date: September 20
Place: Port-au-Prince, Haiti
Event: hurricane
Property damage: many houses damaged by wind, rain, flooding, and landslides
Casualties: hundreds homeless and missing

Partner B
from Apex News
Date: September 14
Place: Italy
Event: earthquake, magnitude 5.5
Property damage: slight in newer buildings; moderate in older ones
Casualties: 12 injuries, none severe or life-threatening

“There was a 5.5 magnitude earthquake in Italy.”

STEP 2. GROUP WORK. Choose one of the following historic disasters. Find information about it on the Internet, at a library, or in a bookstore. Write the information on your notepad. Then present the information to the class.

The San Francisco earthquake of 1906 (U.S.)
The Mount Saint Helens volcanic eruption in 1980 (U.S.)
The Bam earthquake of 2003 (Iran)
The tsunami of 2004 (Indian Ocean)
One of your choice: ______

place and date:
event:
casualties:
destruction:

STEP 3. WRITING. On a separate sheet of paper, write about the disaster you researched.

UNIT 6 CHECKPOINT

A LISTENING COMPREHENSION. Listen to the report. Then check the eight disasters mentioned. Listen again if necessary.

The 10 Most Deadly Natural Disasters of the 20TH Century

		Place	Year	Disaster	Killed
☐	1	worldwide	1917	epidemic	20,000,000
☐	2	Soviet Union	1932	famine	5,000,000
☐	3	China	1931	flood	3,700,000
☐	4	China	1928	drought	3,000,000
☐	5	worldwide	1914	epidemic	3,000,000
☐	6	Soviet Union	1917	epidemic	2,500,000
☐	7	China	1959	flood	2,000,000
☐	8	India	1920	epidemic	2,000,000
☐	9	Bangladesh	1943	famine	1,900,000
☐	10	China	1909	epidemic	1,500,000

SOURCE: CRED (Center for Research on the Epidemiology of Disasters)

TOP NOTCH **SONG**
"Lucky to Be Alive"
Lyrics on last book page.

TOP NOTCH **PROJECT**
Check the global weather report in the newspaper or on the Internet. Report storms and other weather. emergencies around the globe.

TOP NOTCH **WEBSITE**
For Unit 6 online activities, visit the *Top Notch* Companion Website at www.longman.com/topnotch.

B Complete each statement with the name of the event.

drought
flood
landslide
epidemic
hurricane

1. In a _____, mud and soil cover the houses and can bury whole towns.
2. A widespread event in which many people become sick with the same illness is an _____ .
3. A _____ occurs when water from a river enters houses and roads.
4. A storm with high winds and rain is a _____ .
5. When there is no rain for a long period of time, a _____ is said to occur.

C Complete each indirect statement or question. Use said or told.

1. They _____ me to call the office in the morning.
2. He _____ the storm was awful.
3. The students _____ the test had been very difficult.
4. Who _____ us to get a flu shot?
5. We _____ the children to prepare for the storm.

D WRITING. On a separate sheet of paper, write about one of the following subjects:

1. How to prepare for an emergency
2. What to do when an emergency occurs
3. How location, magnitude, timing, and building construction affect the amount of destruction caused by an earthquake

TUESDAY
TOMORROW'S WEATHER...
TROPICAL STORM EXPECTED, WITH HIGH WINDS, DAMAGING RAIN, POSSIBLE FLOODING NEAR COASTAL AREAS
HEADLINES
WEDNESDAY
THE SHELTER IS NOW OPEN AND ACCEPTING PEOPLE FROM AREAS NEAR THE BEACH

Unit Wrap-Up

- **Narration.** Tell the story in the pictures. Who do you think the people are? What does the report say about the weather?
- **Social Language.** Create a conversation between the two men on Tuesday.

Now I can ...

- ☐ convey a message.
- ☐ report news.
- ☐ prepare for an emergency.
- ☐ describe natural disasters.

UNIT 7

Books and Magazines

UNIT GOALS

1 Recommend a book
2 Explain where you learned something
3 Discuss the quality of reading materials
4 Describe your reading habits

TOPIC PREVIEW. Look at the bookstore website. Which books look the most interesting to you? Why?

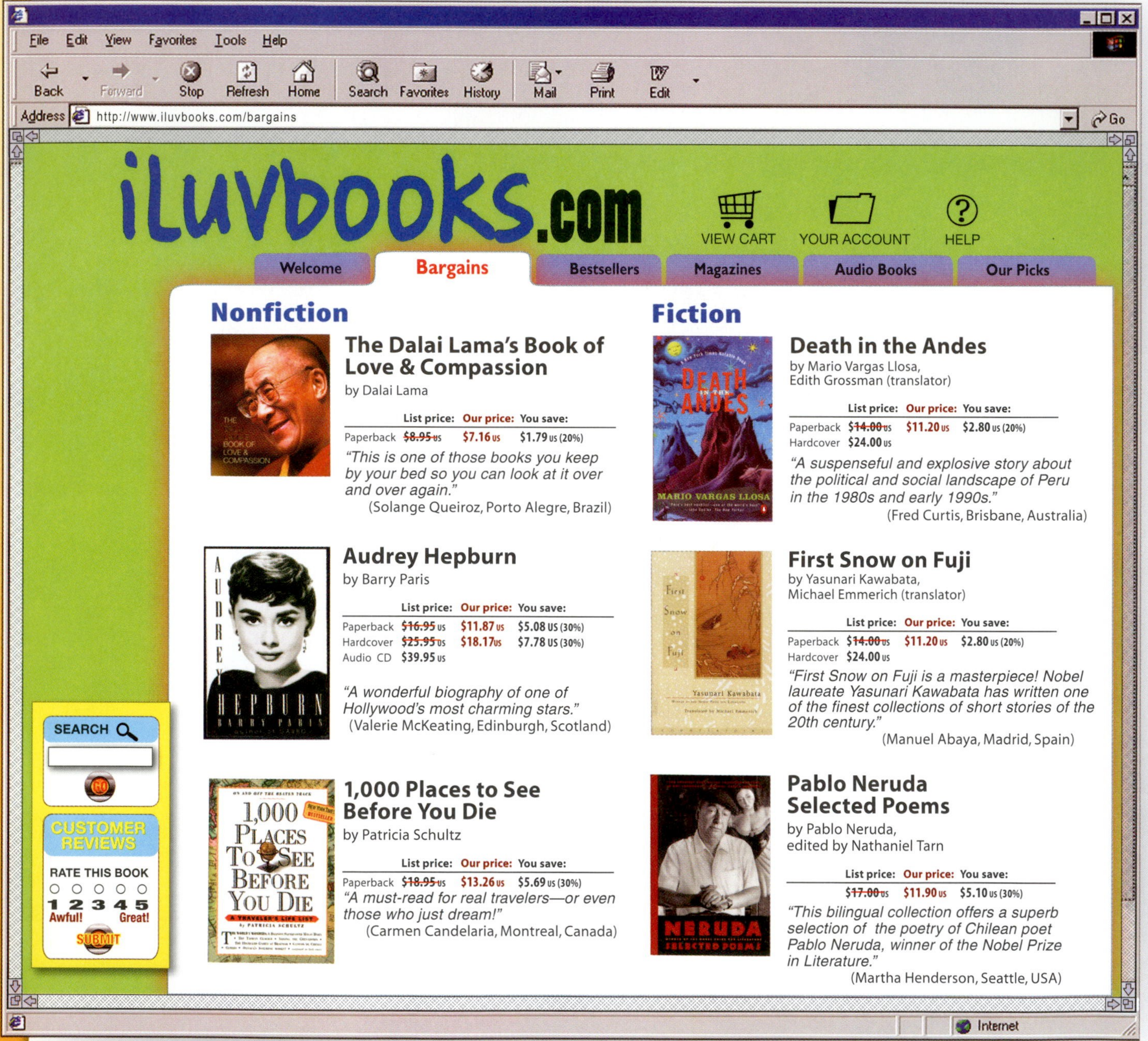

File Edit View Favorites Tools Help

Back Forward Stop Refresh Home Search Favorites History Mail Print Edit

Address http://www.iluvbooks.com/bargains

iLuvbooks.com

VIEW CART YOUR ACCOUNT HELP

Welcome | Bargains | Bestsellers | Magazines | Audio Books | Our Picks

Nonfiction

The Dalai Lama's Book of Love & Compassion

by Dalai Lama

	List price:	Our price:	You save:
Paperback	~~$8.95 US~~	$7.16 US	$1.79 US (20%)

"This is one of those books you keep by your bed so you can look at it over and over again."
(Solange Queiroz, Porto Alegre, Brazil)

Audrey Hepburn

by Barry Paris

	List price:	Our price:	You save:
Paperback	~~$16.95 US~~	$11.87 US	$5.08 US (30%)
Hardcover	~~$25.95 US~~	$18.17 US	$7.78 US (30%)
Audio CD	$39.95 US		

"A wonderful biography of one of Hollywood's most charming stars."
(Valerie McKeating, Edinburgh, Scotland)

1,000 Places to See Before You Die

by Patricia Schultz

	List price:	Our price:	You save:
Paperback	~~$18.95 US~~	$13.26 US	$5.69 US (30%)

"A must-read for real travelers—or even those who just dream!"
(Carmen Candelaria, Montreal, Canada)

Fiction

Death in the Andes

by Mario Vargas Llosa,
Edith Grossman (translator)

	List price:	Our price:	You save:
Paperback	~~$14.00 US~~	$11.20 US	$2.80 US (20%)
Hardcover	$24.00 US		

"A suspenseful and explosive story about the political and social landscape of Peru in the 1980s and early 1990s."
(Fred Curtis, Brisbane, Australia)

First Snow on Fuji

by Yasunari Kawabata,
Michael Emmerich (translator)

	List price:	Our price:	You save:
Paperback	~~$14.00 US~~	$11.20 US	$2.80 US (20%)
Hardcover	$24.00 US		

"First Snow on Fuji is a masterpiece! Nobel laureate Yasunari Kawabata has written one of the finest collections of short stories of the 20th century."
(Manuel Abaya, Madrid, Spain)

Pablo Neruda Selected Poems

by Pablo Neruda,
edited by Nathaniel Tarn

List price:	Our price:	You save:
~~$17.00 US~~	$11.90 US	$5.10 US (30%)

"This bilingual collection offers a superb selection of the poetry of Chilean poet Pablo Neruda, winner of the Nobel Prize in Literature."
(Martha Henderson, Seattle, USA)

SEARCH GO

CUSTOMER REVIEWS

RATE THIS BOOK
1 2 3 4 5
Awful! Great!
SUBMIT

Internet

DISCUSSION. Do you prefer fiction or nonfiction? Have you ever read a book in English? A magazine? A newspaper? If not, would you like to?

C SOUND BITES. Read along silently as you listen to a natural conversation.

JANET: Hey, Lucy! Looking for anything special?
LUCY: Janet! No, I'm just browsing. What are <u>you</u> up to?
JANET: I'm picking up some gardening magazines for my mom. She can't get enough of them. So are you reading anything good these days?
LUCY: Well, I've got a book of poetry on my night table, but I just can't seem to get into it. I guess poetry just doesn't turn me on.
JANET: Have you read the new John Grisham?
LUCY: No, actually, I haven't. I didn't know he had a new book out.
JANET: Well, I can't put it down. It's a real page-turner.
LUCY: Thanks for the tip. I think I'll get that.
JANET: Don't bother. I'm just about finished. If you can wait till the end of the week, I'll lend it to you.

D UNDERSTANDING FROM CONTEXT. Classify each of the following expressions by its meaning. Explain your choices.

I can't put it down. I can't get into it. I can't get enough of it.
I'm really into it. It doesn't turn me on. It's a real page-turner.

I like it.	I don't like it.

E IN OTHER WORDS. Explain the meaning of the following expressions from the conversation.

1. "I'm just browsing."
2. "Thanks for the tip."
3. "I'll lend it to you."

WHAT ABOUT YOU?

What percentage of your reading time do you spend on the following materials? (Make sure it adds up to 100%!)

	%
magazines	______
newspapers	______
websites	______
fiction	______
nonfiction	______
other	______

LESSON

1 Recommend a Book

CONVERSATION MODEL Read and listen.

A: What's that you're reading?
B: It's a Hemingway novel, *The Old Man and the Sea*.
A: I've always wanted to read that! Is it any good?
B: Oh, I'd highly recommend it. It's a real page-turner.
A: Do you mind if I borrow it when you're done?
B: Not at all.

Rhythm and intonation practice

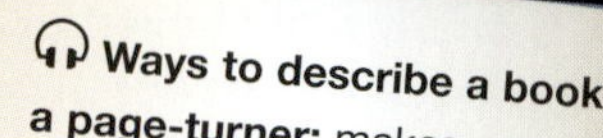

Ways to describe a book

- **a page-turner:** makes you want to keep reading it
- **a cliffhanger:** exciting; you don't know what will happen next
- **hard to follow:** difficult to understand

- **a bestseller:** very popular; lots of copies have been sold
- **a fast read:** not very challenging, but enjoyable
- **trash:** very poor quality

A GRAMMAR. Noun clauses: embedded questions

You can "embed" a question in a larger statement.
Begin embedded yes / no questions with if or whether.

Yes / no questions	Embedded yes / no questions
Is it any good?	I don't know **if** (or **whether**) **it's any good**.
Did he like the novel?	I wonder **if** (or **whether**) **he liked the novel**.
Have you finished the book?	Could you tell me **if** (or **whether**) **you've finished the book**?
Can I borrow John's magazine?	Would you mind asking John **if** (or **whether**) **I could borrow his magazine**?

Use a question word to begin embedded information questions.

Information questions	Embedded information questions
What's the book about?	Tell me **what the book's about**.
Why did you decide to read it?	Tell me **why you decided to read it**.
Who's the author?	I wonder **who the author is**.
Who is it written for?	I wonder **who it's written for**.
Whose book is this?	I'd like to know **whose book this is**.
When was it written?	Do you know **when it was written**?
Where does it take place?	Do you know **where it takes place**?

BE CAREFUL!
Use normal (not inverted) word order in embedded questions.
Do you know **who** the author **is**?
NOT Do you know ~~who is~~ the author?

PAGES G11–G12
For more ...

B Use each question to complete the embedded questions.

1. Does she like to read? I wonder ____________________.
2. Where did you get this magazine? Can you tell me ____________________?
3. Is he a Garcia Marquez fan? I've been wondering ____________________.
4. Why do you never read fiction? I'm curious ____________________.
5. Who told you about this author? I was wondering ____________________.
6. When did you first hear about that website? I'd really like to know ____________________.

 VOCABULARY. Types of books. Listen and practice.

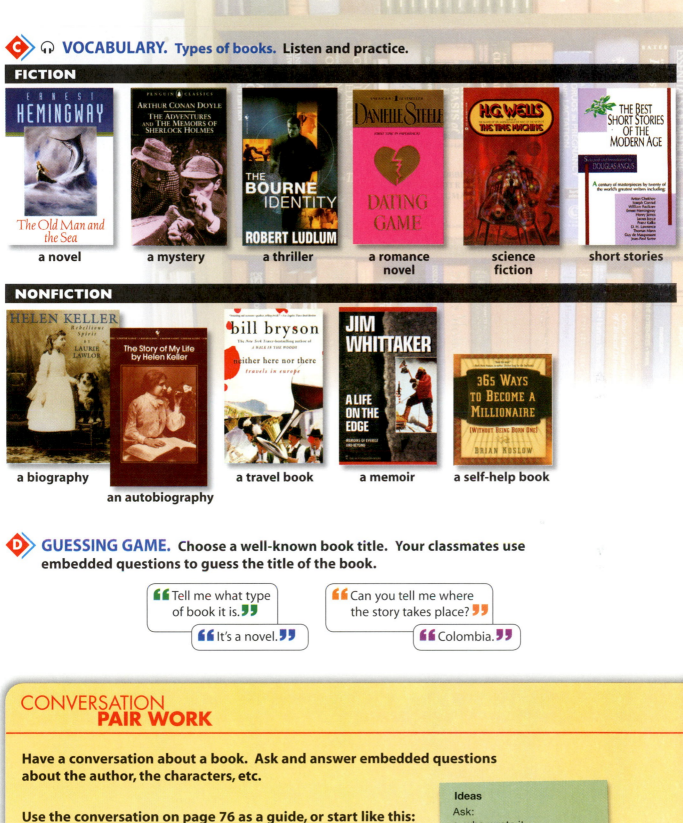

FICTION

a novel

a mystery

a thriller

a romance novel

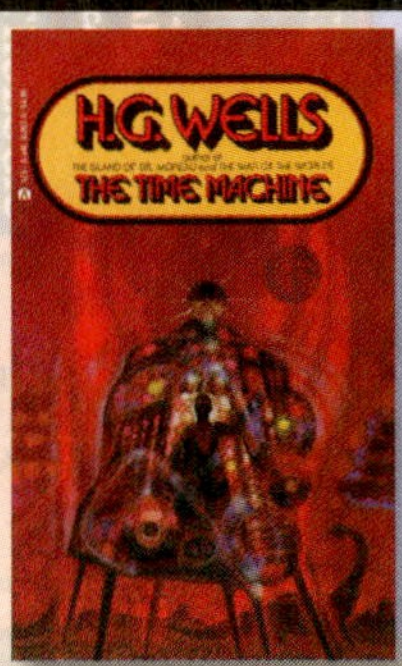

science fiction

short stories

NONFICTION

a biography

an autobiography

a travel book

a memoir

a self-help book

D GUESSING GAME. Choose a well-known book title. Your classmates use embedded questions to guess the title of the book.

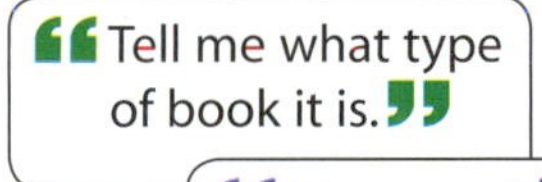

"Tell me what type of book it is."

"It's a novel."

"Can you tell me where the story takes place?"

"Colombia."

CONVERSATION PAIR WORK

Have a conversation about a book. Ask and answer embedded questions about the author, the characters, etc.

Use the conversation on page 76 as a guide, or start like this:

A: What are you reading these days?

B: ______ ...

Ideas

Ask:

- who wrote it
- what it's about
- where it takes place
- who it's written for
- when it was written
- if it's any good

LESSON

Explain Where You Learned Something

CONVERSATION MODEL Read and listen.

A: What incredible bread! Did you make it?
B: Yes, thanks! I learned how in the latest issue of *Home* magazine.
A: I didn't know they had recipes.
B: Would you like to borrow a copy?
A: I don't think so. I'm all thumbs!

Rhythm and intonation practice

GRAMMAR. Noun clauses as direct objects

A noun clause can be the direct object of a verb of mental activity.

	noun clause
I didn't know	**that *Home* magazine had recipes**.
I think	**that they have great recipes**.

When the noun clause is a direct object, the word that is often omitted. There is no change in meaning.

I didn't know ~~that~~ you read *Home* magazine.
I hope ~~that~~ the store has the latest issue.

As in reported speech, the tense in the noun clause often changes to support meaning.

I hope we aren't too late. I **hoped** we **weren't** too late.
I think she finished the book. I **thought** she **had finished** the book.

In short answers, use so to replace the noun clause after the verbs think, believe, guess, and hope.

A: Do you have the latest issue of *Car* magazine?
B: I think **so**. / I don't think **so**.
I believe **so**. / I don't believe **so**.
(so = that I have the latest issue.)

PAGES G12–G13
For more …

BE CAREFUL!
I hope so. / I hope **not**.
NOT ~~I don't hope so.~~
I guess so. / I guess **not**.
NOT ~~I don't guess so.~~

PRONUNCIATION. Sentence stress in short answers with think, hope, guess, or believe. Listen and repeat.

1. Does your husband like reading mysteries? **I THINK so.**
2. Has Jack finished that travel book yet? **I don't THINK so.**
3. Do you think that novel will be good? **I HOPE so.**
4. Did your sister enjoy that romance novel? **I GUESS so.**
5. Is the ending of that story interesting? **I beLIEVE so.**

C **Change each statement to a direct object noun clause, changing verb tenses if necessary.**

1. The latest issue of *Car* magazine has information on hybrid cars.
   I think the latest issue of Car has information on hybrid cars.
2. That article on knitting sweaters in *Home* magazine is great.
   She thought ______________________________.
3. *PC Magazine* is pretty inexpensive.
   Most people believe ______________________________.
4. There aren't any articles about fixing furniture in *Handy* magazine this month.
   I guess ______________________________.
5. There's an article about Nelson Mandela in this week's *Weekly News*.
   We hope ______________________________.
6. Nancy bought last week's issue of *World Affairs* before the new one came out.
   Frank thought ______________________________.

D **PAIR WORK.** **Ask and answer yes / no questions about your partner's future plans. Respond with short answers, using think, believe, hope, or guess.**

"Are you going to go out of town this weekend?"

"I think so!"

CONVERSATION PAIR WORK

Role-play a conversation about where you learned to do something. Use the photos and magazine covers here and the conversation model on page 78 as a guide.

"What a beautiful scarf!"

"What amazing speakers!"

Happy Home

curtains

a scarf

a bookshelf

speakers

LESSON

3 Discuss the Quality of Reading Materials

A **READING WARM-UP.** **Do you read comics? Does anyone in your family read them? Do you think they're good reading material?**

B **READING.** **Read the article. In what country are comics the most popular?**

COMICS *trash or treasure?*

In Japan, they call them *manga*; in Latin America, *historietas*; in Italy, *fumetti*; in Brazil, *historia em quadrinhos*; and in the U.S., comics. But no matter what you call them, comics are a favorite source of reading pleasure in many parts of the world.

In case you're wondering how popular comics are, the bestselling comic title in the U.S. sells about 4.5 million copies a year. All of Mexico's comic titles together sell over 7 million copies a week. But Japan is by far the leading publisher of comics in the world. *Manga* account for nearly 40 percent of all the books and magazines published in Japan each year. And few magazines of any kind in the world can match this number: *Shonen Jump*, the leading comic title, has a circulation of 6.5 million copies per week!

Ever since comics first appeared, there have been people who have criticized them. In the 1940s and 50s, many people believed that comics were immoral and that they caused bad behavior among young people. Even today, many question whether young people should read them at all. They argue that reading comics encourages bad reading habits.

But some educators see comics as a way to get teenagers to choose reading instead of television and video games. And because of the art, a number of educators have argued that comics are a great way to get children to think creatively. More recent research has suggested that the combination of visuals and text in comics may be one reason young people handle computers and related software so easily.

In many places, comics have been a convenient way to communicate social or political information. For example, in the 1990s, comics were used by the Brazilian health ministry to communicate information about AIDS.

In Japan, the Education Ministry calls comics "a part of Japan's national culture, recognized and highly regarded abroad." Comics are increasingly being used for educational purposes, and many publishers there see them as a useful way of teaching history and other subjects.

No matter how you view them, comics remain a guilty pleasure for millions worldwide.

▲ Spider-Man® is one of the world's most recognizable and celebrated comic superheroes. Fifteen million Spider-Man comics are sold each year in 75 countries and in 22 languages, and he appears in 500 newspapers worldwide.

◀ In Japan, train station newsstands do a booming business selling *manga* during rush hour. And for those addicts who must have their *manga* in the middle of the night, automatic vending machines are everywhere.

◀ More comic books are consumed per capita in Mexico than in any other Latin American country.

SOURCES: Associated Press, Ananova News Service, PRNewswire

C **Answer the questions, according to the information in the article.**

1. What are the reasons some people criticize comics?
2. What are some of the possible benefits of comics?
3. Why do some people feel guilty or bad about reading comics?

D **DISCUSSION. Who reads comics in your country? What kinds of stories and characters can you find in comics? What do you think of comics?**

TOP NOTCH INTERACTION • *Trash or treasure?*

STEP 1. PAIR WORK. Complete your notepad with your opinions about different reading materials. Discuss your answers with your partner.

	trash or	treasure?	reasons...
comics	☑	☐	I think they are violent and sexist.

	trash or	treasure?	reasons...
comics	☐	☐	
teen magazines	☐	☐	
fashion magazines	☐	☐	
sports magazines	☐	☐	
movie magazines	☐	☐	
romance novels	☐	☐	
thrillers	☐	☐	
mysteries	☐	☐	
other ________	☐	☐	

STEP 2. DISCUSSION. Choose one type of reading material that you think is trash and one that you think is treasure. Explain your opinions, using specific titles of books, magazines, etc.

NEED HELP? **Here's language you already know:**

Expression of opinion
I think (that)...
In my opinion...
Could you explain why you think (that)... ?
I guess you're saying (that)...

Describing reading materials
I can't put [them] down.
I'm really into [them].
I can't get enough of [them].
They're a fast read.
I can't get into [them].
[They] don't turn me on.

Other types of reading materials
science fiction
biographies
autobiographies
self-help books
novels
travel books
memoirs
short stories

LESSON 4

Describe Your Reading Habits

VOCABULARY. Some ways to enjoy books, magazines, and newspapers.
Listen and practice.

curl up with a book

read aloud to someone

collect clippings

do puzzles

skim through a newspaper

listen to books on tape

Complete the sentences. Use the new vocabulary in the correct form.

1. Jerry has a lot of great recipes. He loves to __________ from newspaper cooking articles.
2. Martin enjoys grabbing a pencil and __________. It helps him learn new words and pass the time.
3. Nancy finds it really convenient to __________ rather than reading them. She can do it while she's driving.
4. It gives Tom great pleasure to __________ to his kids before they go to bed.
5. When it's late at night, Beatrice likes nothing more than to __________ a fashion magazine and a cup of tea before she goes to sleep.
6. Kate is so busy she doesn't really have a lot of time to read. She just __________ things, never reading anything from start to finish.

LISTENING COMPREHENSION. Listen to each person talk about reading habits. Then read the chart and listen again. Check the reading habits of each person.

- ☐ enjoys reading newspapers
- ☐ prefers reading in the park
- ☐ likes to curl up in bed with a newspaper
- ☐ reads in the bathroom
- ☐ is into historical novels
- ☐ collects magazine clippings
- ☐ enjoys skimming through magazines

Ignacio Saralegui
Buenos Aires, Argentina

Su Yomei
Taipei, Taiwan

- ☐ likes to curl up with a good book
- ☐ reads in the kitchen
- ☐ likes to read in coffee shops
- ☐ enjoys skimming through magazines
- ☐ enjoys doing puzzles
- ☐ is into movie magazines
- ☐ collects newspaper clippings

SOURCE: authentic *Top Notch* interviews

TOP NOTCH INTERACTION • *What are your reading habits?*

STEP 1. PAIR WORK. **Interview your partner. Write your partner's answers.**

1. Tell me where you like to do most of your reading.

2. When do you like to read?

3. Do you enjoy skimming through magazines, books, or other reading materials? (Explain.)

4. Do you like collecting newspaper or magazine clippings? (From where? What do you do with them?)

5. Do you like to read aloud to other people or have other people read aloud to you?

6. Do you ever listen to books on tape? (Why or why not?)

7. What types of books do you like to read?

8. What are your favorite books of all time?

9. Tell me who your favorite authors are.

STEP 2. **Tell your class about your partner's reading habits.**

"Ellen told me that she prefers to read in bed before she goes to sleep."

STEP 3. WRITING. **Describe your <u>own</u> reading habits.**

FREE PRACTICE

UNIT 7 CHECKPOINT

A **LISTENING COMPREHENSION.** **Listen carefully to the conversations and write the type of book each person is discussing. Then listen again and check how the person feels about the book.**

	type of book	likes it	doesn't like it
Conversation 1	________	☐	☐
Conversation 2	________	☐	☐
Conversation 3	________	☐	☐
Conversation 4	________	☐	☐

B **Complete each statement with a type of book.**

1. A novel about people falling in love is usually called a ________ .
2. A book about a famous person is called a ________ .
3. A book that a famous person writes about his or her own life is called an ________ .
4. A very exciting novel about a dangerous situation can be called a ________ .
5. Books that are about factual information are called ________ .
6. A strange fictional story about the future is called ________ .

C **Use each question to complete the embedded question.**

1. Where does the story take place?
   Could you tell me ______________________________?
2. Who is the main character in the novel?
   I was wondering ______________________________ .
3. How much was that German newspaper?
   I can't remember ______________________________ .
4. How do you say this in English?
   I was wondering ______________________________ .
5. What does this word mean?
   Could you explain ______________________________?

D **WRITING.** **Write a review about a book you've read. Say who the author is. Describe where it takes place, who the characters are, and what it's about. Recommend it or warn the reader to avoid it.**

***TOP NOTCH* WEBSITE**
For Unit 7 online activities, visit the *Top Notch* Companion Website at www.longman.com/topnotch.

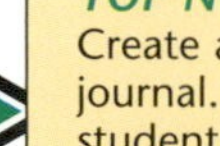

***TOP NOTCH* PROJECT**
Create a literary review journal. Include reviews students have written about different types of reading material.

Unit Wrap-Up

- **Grammar.** Look at the picture for a minute; then close your book. Answer your partner's questions with short answers, using think, believe, or guess.

  A: *Is someone skimming through magazines?*
  B: *I think so.*

- **Social Language.** Create conversations for the people.

  A: *What a great sweater.*
  B: *Thanks . . .*

Now I can . . .

- ☐ recommend a book.
- ☐ explain where I learned something.
- ☐ discuss the quality of reading materials.
- ☐ describe my reading habits.

UNIT 8

Inventions and Technology

UNIT GOALS

1 Describe an innovation
2 Accept responsibility for a mistake
3 Evaluate inventions
4 Discuss the impact of key inventions in history

A TOPIC PREVIEW. Do you consider the wheel to be the most important mechanical invention in history? What other modern uses of the wheel can you name?

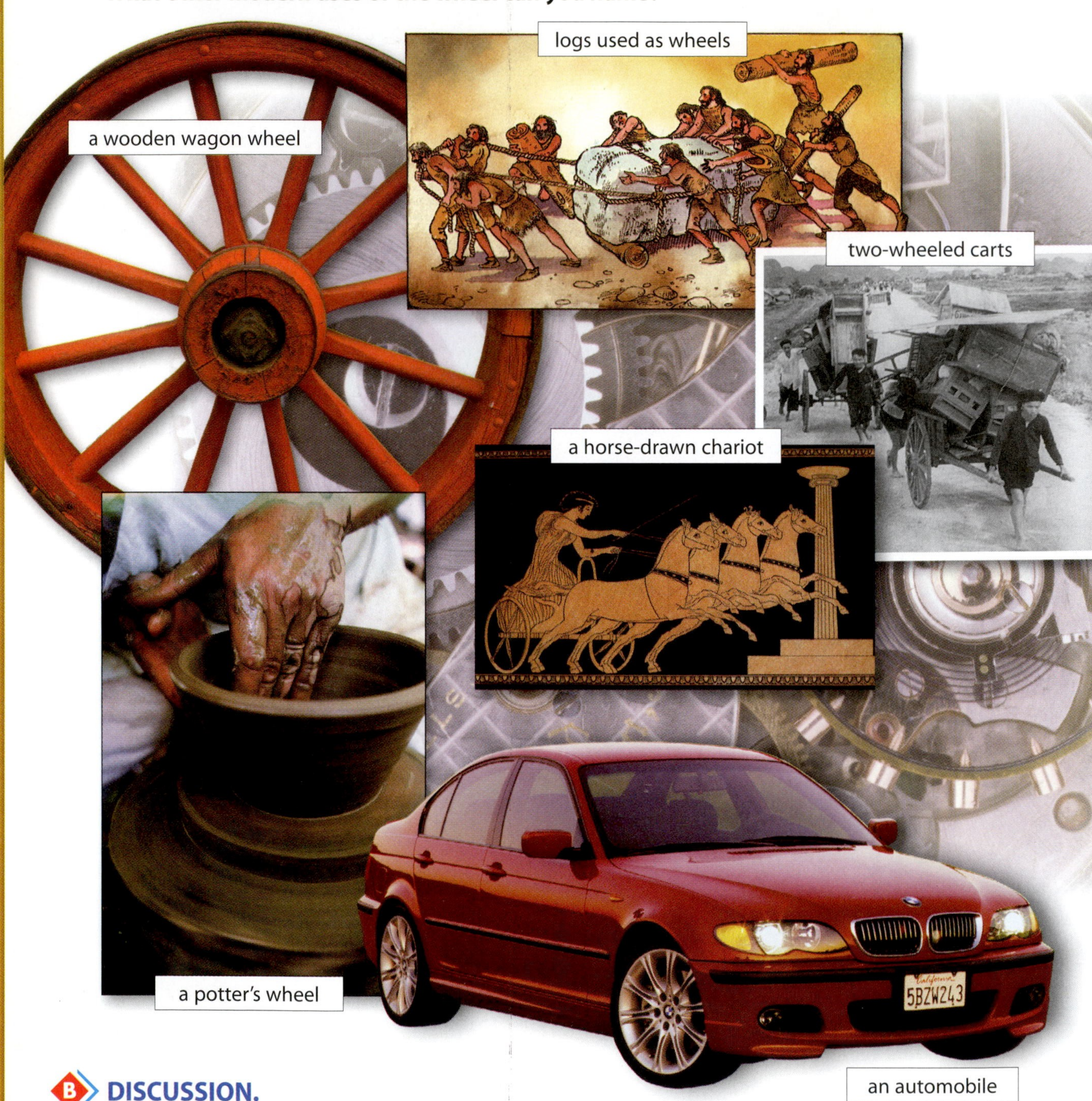

B DISCUSSION.

1. What difficulties did people have before the invention of the wheel?
2. How did the wheel change the lives of people?

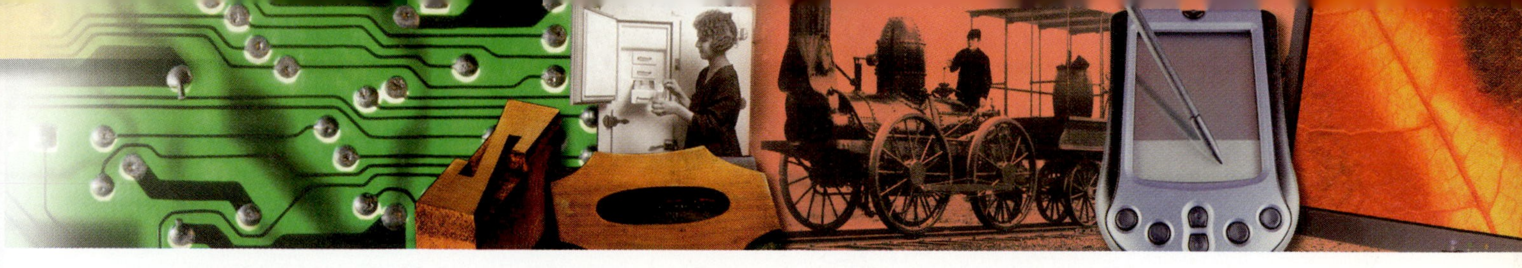

C SOUND BITES. Read along silently as you listen to a natural conversation.

LILIAN: Where did you get all those mosquito bites?

MARIAN: On our camping trip. The bugs were horrendous. I tried everything, but I still got eaten alive! Don't you wish someone would invent something for mosquitoes that works?

LILIAN: Where have you been? They have!

MARIAN: No way!

LILIAN: Yeah. It's this thing you put on your wrist, and mosquitoes quit bugging you. It really works.

MARIAN: I don't believe it. If I'd known that, I would have gotten one before I left.

D UNDERSTANDING FROM CONTEXT. Find words and expressions in the conversation. Then use each one in a sentence.

1. Find a word that means "terrible." ____________
2. Find an expression that means "The bugs bit me a lot." ____________
3. Find a word that means "bothering" or "annoying." ____________

E PAIR WORK. With a partner, answer the questions. Explain your answers.

1. What does Lilian mean when she asks Marian, "Where have you been?"
2. What does Marian mean when she says, "No way!"

an early television, 1950

WHAT ABOUT **YOU?**

The following machines were invented in the twentieth century. Rank them in order of importance from 1 to 5, with 1 being the most important:

☐ the computer ☐ the airplane ☐ the automobile ☐ the telephone ☐ the television

DISCUSSION. **Explain your rankings.**

LESSON

1 Discuss a New Product

CONVERSATION MODEL Read and listen.

A: I need a new coffee maker. Do you think I should get the Brew Rite? It's on sale at TechnoMart.

B: That depends. How much are they selling it for?

A: $75.

B: Definitely. That's a great price. If I needed a coffee maker, I'd buy one too. It's top of the line.

Rhythm and intonation practice

A VOCABULARY. Describing manufactured products. Listen and practice.

Uses new technology	Offers high quality	Uses new ideas
high-tech	high-end	innovative
state-of-the-art	top-of-the-line	revolutionary
cutting-edge	first-rate	novel

B GRAMMAR. Factual and unreal conditional sentences: review

Present factual conditionals: Use the simple present tense in both clauses.
If you **make** a lot of coffee, you **need** a good coffee maker.

Future factual conditionals: Use the simple present tense in the if clause. Use the future with will or be going to in the result clause.
If they **sell** the Brew Rite for as low a price as the Coffee King, they**'ll sell** a lot of them.

Present unreal conditionals: Use the simple past tense or were in the if clause. Use would in the result clause.
If I **were** you, I **wouldn't buy** it. (unreal condition: I am not you.)
If Teletex **had** a cutting-edge digital camera phone, they **would sell** more. (unreal condition: Teletex doesn't have one.)

BE CAREFUL! Don't use a future form in the if clause.
If I buy it, I'll be happy.
NOT If I ~~will buy~~ it, I'll be happy.

Don't use would in the if clause.
If they knew the best brand, they would get it.
NOT If they ~~would know~~ the best brand, they would get it.

PAGES G13–G14
For more ...

C Practice distinguishing between factual and unreal conditions. Check the statements that describe unreal conditions.

☐ 1. If they see something first-rate, they buy it.
☐ 2. If we take the bus to TechnoMart, we save a lot of time.
☐ 3. If you walked to the theater, you would get there late.
☐ 4. They won't get any phone calls if they don't have their cell phones.
☐ 5. If she were a photographer, she would sell her old camera and buy a new one.

D Complete each present factual conditional sentence.

1. Water ________ (boil) if you ________ (raise) its temperature to 100 degrees.
2. If I ________ (see) something that's really cutting edge, I ________ (want) it.
3. She ________ (grind) her own beans if she ________________ (want) really great coffee.
4. He always ________ (use) state-of-the-art equipment if it ________ (be) available.

E Choose the correct form to complete each future factual conditional sentence.

1. If they ____________ (want / will want) to get there fast, they ____________ (take / will take) the express train.
2. If he ____________ (buys / will buy) the product, the mosquitoes ____________ (don't bite / won't bite).
3. If they ____________ (see / will see) her tomorrow, they ____________ (show / will show) her their new camera phone.
4. ____________________ (Are you going to get / Do you get) the camera phone if they ____________ (offer / will offer) it on sale?

F PAIR WORK. Take turns completing each present unreal conditional in your own way.

1. If I were an inventor, I …
2. If I could go anywhere in the world, …
3. If I needed a car, …

CONVERSATION PAIR WORK

Bring in advertisements for products from a newspaper, or use these ads. Use the vocabulary on page 88 to describe the products. Discuss whether or not to buy them.

Start like this:

A: I need a new _____ . Do you think I should get the _____? …

B: _____ …

Digicon B1X
• cutting-edge technology
• 5.44 megapixel
US $3899
Save $50
US $379
17" LCD Monitor
Teknicon
Micro Scanner
• state-of-the-art
US $199
Strawberry Palmtop SPECIAL BUY
• handheld
• Internet capable
• secure digital
• media card slot
US $99
super special
Digi-Phone
• 2-line digital phone system
US $79

LESSON

2 Accept Responsibility for a Mistake

CONVERSATION MODEL Read and listen.

A: Sorry we're late. We got lost.
B: That's OK. It can happen to anyone.
A: Well, it was entirely my fault. If I had stopped to ask for directions, we would have been on time.
B: Well, better late than never. Please come in. And let me get you something to drink.

Rhythm and intonation practice

A GRAMMAR. The past unreal conditional

Use the past unreal conditional to describe unreal or untrue conditions and results.

If I **had had** a cell phone, I **could have called** for directions. (But I didn't, so I couldn't call.)
She **wouldn't have been** late if she **had checked** the map. (But she didn't, so she was late.)

BE CAREFUL! Don't use would or could in the if clause in the past unreal conditional.

If I ~~would have had~~ a cell phone, I could have called for directions.

Questions and answers

Could they have arrived on time if they had left earlier?	Yes, they could have. / No, they couldn't have.
When would you have arrived if you had taken the train?	At four o'clock.

GRAMMAR BOOSTER
PAGES G14–G15 For more ...

B Choose the meaning of each past unreal conditional sentence.

1. They wouldn't have gone if they hadn't gotten a ticket on the Bullet Train.
   a. They went. b. They didn't go.
2. If we had been there, we would have chosen another kind of transportation.
   a. We were there. b. We weren't there.
3. If you hadn't told them about it, they never would have known.
   a. You told them about it. b. You didn't tell them about it.
4. If someone had explained the directions better, we wouldn't have gotten lost.
   a. We got lost. b. We didn't get lost.

C Choose the correct forms to complete each past unreal conditional sentence.

1. What would you have done if you ______ a phone in your car?
   wouldn't have had / hadn't had
2. If you ______ about the storm, would you have tried to evacuate?
   would have known / had known
3. If the airplane had not been invented, people ______ a way to travel more quickly by land.
   would find / would have found
4. If the flood ______ during the night, many more people ______.
   would have occurred / had occurred
   would have been injured / would be injured

D **PAIR WORK.** **Take turns completing the statements about each headline. Then discuss the actions you would have taken if you had read the headlines.**

Hurricane to Strike Tonight
Floods Expected

YOU If I had seen this, I …

Massive Transportation Strike
Taxis, Buses, Trains Out of Service
Huge Traffic Jams Expected

YOU If I had seen this, I …

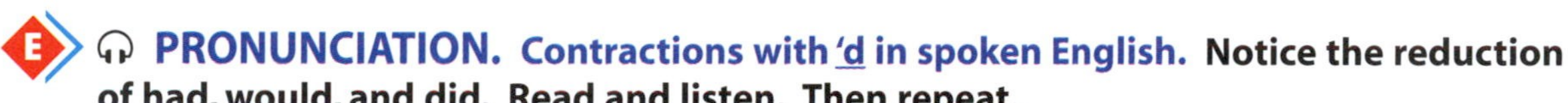

Stores Announce Protest Against Taxes
Half-price Sales Begin Today

YOU If I had seen this, I …

E **PRONUNCIATION.** **Contractions with 'd in spoken English. Notice the reduction of had, would, and did. Read and listen. Then repeat.**

1. If we had had time, we would have stayed. → If we'd /wid/ had time, we would have stayed.
2. Where did you go? → Where'd /wɛrd/ you go?
3. Who did you see? → Who'd /hud/ you see?
4. It would be OK. → It'd /ɪt̬əd/ be OK.

CONVERSATION PAIR WORK

Role-play accepting responsibility for a mistake. Use the past unreal conditional to explain how things could have been different. Accept your partner's apology.

A: Sorry ____.

B: That's OK. ____.

A: Well, it was entirely my fault. If ____ …

Continue the conversation in your own way.

Ideas...

- You were late.
- You forgot someone's birthday.
- You didn't pay a bill on time.
- You forgot to call someone.
- Your own idea: ____

CONTROLLED PRACTICE

LESSON

Evaluate Inventions

A VOCABULARY. Descriptive adjectives. Listen and practice.

low-tech / high-tech

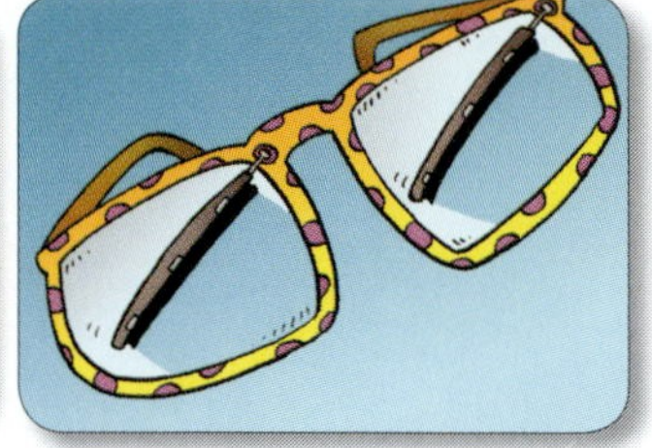
wacky

unique

efficient / inefficient

B LISTENING COMPREHENSION. Listen carefully to people discussing their problems. Write the number of the conversation next to the invention each person should have had.

☐ The Robo-Tiller

☐ The All-Body Umbrella

☐ The Pet Exit

☐ The Vac Bot

C DISCUSSION. Describe each invention with one or more of the adjectives from the vocabulary.

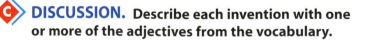

"It's not a novel idea, but the Pet Exit is both low-tech and efficient. It doesn't need electronics or machinery."

STEP 1. **Check the boxes to show where you think new inventions are needed. Then complete the chart with more information about each invention.**

	New invention	Why people would want it
home and car		
☑ for the car	a wake-up alarm	so you don't fall asleep while driving
☐ for organizing		
☐ for cooking		
☐ for raising children		
☐ for pets		
☐ for cleaning		
☐ for relaxing		
office		
☐ for writing		
☐ for organizing papers		
☐ for training staff		
☐ for communicating		
☐ for eating lunch or snacking		
English class		
☐ for learning new words and grammar		
☐ for getting more speaking practice		
☐ for preparing to take tests		
☐ for reading faster		

STEP 2. **PAIR WORK.** **Choose one area and invent something. It can be wacky, low-tech, high-tech, or even impossible! Name your invention. On a separate sheet of paper, draw a picture of it or write a description of it.**

STEP 3. **DISCUSSION.** **Tell the class about your invention. Explain what would happen if you had one now. Explain what you could have done if you'd had one in the past.**

NEED HELP? **Here's language you already know:**

Descriptive adjectives

top-of-the-line
high-tech
high-end
state-of-the-art
cutting-edge
low-tech
first-rate
innovative
wacky
practical
unique
efficient
inefficient
novel
revolutionary

Factual and unreal conditionals

Don't you wish someone would invent something for ____?
If I had a ____, I would be able to ____.
If I had had a ____, I would have been able to ____.

LESSON

Discuss the Impact of Key Inventions in History

A **READING WARM-UP.** **In what ways did people communicate words and ideas to each other before the invention of the telegraph, the telephone, the radio, and the computer?**

B **READING.** **Read about the invention of printing. How do you think this invention changed the world?**

The Printing Press

ladle for pouring hot metal

Until the 6th or 7th century, all books had to be written by hand.

If you asked a large number of people what the most important invention has been, many would say the printing press. Others might say the wheel. But even though it's debatable whether the appearance of the printing press affected the course of history more than the wheel, the printing press ranks within the top two or three inventions in history.

Long before the telephone, the television, the radio, and the computer, the written word was the only way to communicate ideas to people too far away to talk with. Until the sixth or seventh century, all books had to be written by hand. Creating a book was difficult, and in comparison with today, very few books existed. Therefore, very few people read books.

In the sixth and seventh centuries, the Japanese and Chinese invented a way to print pages by carving characters and pictures on wooden, ivory, or clay blocks. They would put ink on the blocks and then press paper onto the ink, printing a page from the block. This process is called letterpress printing. The invention of letterpress printing was a great advance in communication because each block could be inked many times and many copies of each page could be made. Many books could now be made. Therefore, many people could read the same book.

Later, in the 11th century, another great advance occurred. The Chinese invented "movable" type. Each character was made as a separate block which could be used many times in many texts. This meant that pages could be created by putting together individual characters rather than having to have whole pages carved. Movable type was much more efficient than the earlier Japanese and Chinese print blocks because books could be created much more quickly by people with less skill.

In Europe, movable type was used for the first time in the 15th century. And there, Johannes Gutenberg invented typecasting, a way to make movable type much more quickly, by melting metal and pouring it into the forms of the letters. This greatly increased the speed of printing, and eventually made books available to many more people.

carved print blocks

SOURCE: Eyewitness Books: *Invention*. By Lionel Bender, Alfred A. Knopf, New York, © 1991.

DISCUSSION.

1. How would life have been different if printing hadn't been invented?
2. In what ways do we communicate "in writing" today?
3. What makes an invention important? What do you think are the top two or three inventions in history?

TOP NOTCH INTERACTION • *It's the greatest invention since the wheel!*

STEP 1. PAIR WORK. On your notepads, write your own ideas about how life changed as a result of each of these inventions. Then rank the four inventions in order of importance.

2000 B.C.: The plow loosens and turns the soil so crops can be planted efficiently.

1802: The steam locomotive permits transportation of products over long distances by train.

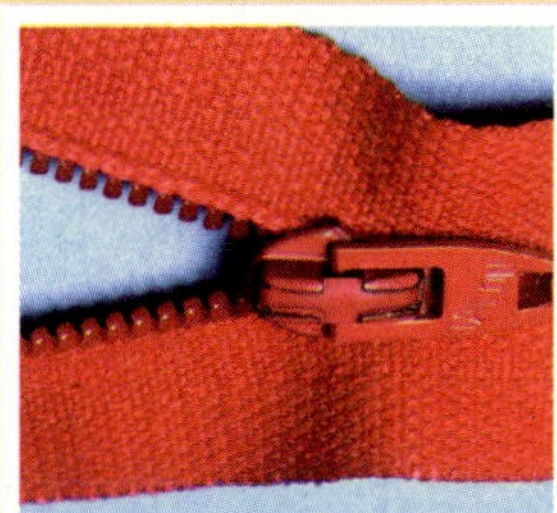

1914: The modern zipper permits the opening and closing of clothes without buttons and buttonholes.

1920s: The electric refrigerator keeps food fresh.

	Life before	Life after
the plow:		
the train:		
the zipper:		
the refrigerator:		

"After the plow was invented, farmers could plant large areas in a short time. Then they could plant enough food to sell to other people."

STEP 2. GROUP WORK. Choose one of the inventions above or another invention. Present a report to your classmates about the impact the invention had in history.

FREE PRACTICE

UNIT 8 CHECKPOINT

A **LISTENING COMPREHENSION.** **Listen to the people talking about new products. Match the name of the product and the adjective that best describes it.**

Products	Adjectives
____ 1. The Ultraphone	a. cutting-edge
____ 2. Dinner-from-a-distance	b. efficient
____ 3. Kinder-TV	c. unique
____ 4. Ten Years Off	d. top-of-the-line

B **Check the statement that is true for each situation.**

1. We wouldn't have gotten lost if we had called in advance for directions.
   - ☐ We called and we got lost.
   - ☐ We didn't call and we got lost.
   - ☐ We called and we didn't get lost.
   - ☐ We didn't call and we didn't get lost.
2. If the salesman were here, he would explain how the Omni works.
   - ☐ The salesman is here, so he can explain how the Omni works.
   - ☐ The salesman is here, so he can't explain how the Omni works.
   - ☐ The salesman isn't here, but he can explain how the Omni works.
   - ☐ The salesman isn't here, so he can't explain how the Omni works.
3. If Laura had bought the Ultraphone, she would have already sent those e-mails.
   - ☐ Laura bought the Ultraphone and she has already sent those e-mails.
   - ☐ Laura didn't buy the Ultraphone and she hasn't sent those e-mails yet.
   - ☐ Laura bought the Ultraphone and she hasn't sent those e-mails yet.
   - ☐ Laura didn't buy the Ultraphone and she has already sent those e-mails.

C **Complete each conditional sentence.**

1. If I had a very fast car, ____________________.
2. Most people would look better if ____________________.
3. Will you buy a new car next year if ____________________?
4. If I had been born before there were cars, ____________________.

D **WRITING.** **Choose one of the following inventions. Write about how it changed life and what would have happened if it had not been invented.**

- the telephone
- the washing machine
- the microwave oven
- the computer

***TOP NOTCH* SONG**
"Reinvent the Wheel"
Lyrics on last book page.

***TOP NOTCH* PROJECT**
Choose an invention appearing during your own lifetime that has changed your life. Make a presentation to the class about the invention.

***TOP NOTCH* WEBSITE**
For Unit 8 online activities, visit the *Top Notch* Companion Website at www.longman.com/topnotch.

Unit Wrap-Up

- **Vocabulary.** Talk about the items in the store, using adjectives to describe them.
- **Grammar.** Complete the statements, using the factual and unreal conditional. Then make more statements.
  If she buys the . . .
  If they bought the . . .
  If Dan hadn't bought the . . .
- **Social Language.** Create conversations for the people.

Now I can . . .

- ☐ describe an innovation.
- ☐ accept responsibility for a mistake.
- ☐ evaluate inventions.
- ☐ discuss the impact of key inventions in history.

UNIT 9

Controversial Issues

UNIT GOALS

1. Ask if it's OK to discuss a topic
2. Discuss controversial issues politely
3. Propose solutions to global problems
4. Debate the pros and cons of issues

A TOPIC PREVIEW. Read the dictionary definitions of some political terms. Then listen and practice.

con-sti-tu-tion /ˌkɑnstəˈtuʃən/ *n.* a set of basic laws and principles that a democratic country is governed by, which cannot easily be changed by the political party in power

de-moc-ra-cy /dɪˈmɑkrəsi/ *n.* **1** a system of government in which every citizen in the country can vote to elect its government officials **2** a country that allows its people to elect its government officials

dic-ta-tor-ship /dɪkˈteɪt̬ɚˌʃɪp/ *n.* government by a ruler who has complete power

e-lec-tion /ɪˈlɛkʃən/ *n.* an occasion when people vote to choose someone for an official position

gov-ern-ment /ˈgʌvɚmənt, ˈgʌvɚnmənt/ *n.* the group of people who govern a country or state: *the French government*

mon-ar-chy /ˈmɑnɚki/ *n.* **1** the system in which a country is ruled by a king or queen **2** a country that is ruled by a king or queen

pol-i-tics /ˈpɑləˌtɪks/ *n.* **1** ideas and activities that are concerned with gaining or using power in a country: *Brock's been involved in city politics since college.* | *Politics doesn't interest me much.* **2** the profession of being a politician: *Flynn retired from politics in 1986.* **3** [plural] the activities of people who are concerned with gaining personal advantage within a group: *I'm tired of dealing with all the office politics.* **4** [plural] someone's political beliefs and opinions: *I don't agree with Michael's politics, but he's sure a nice guy.*

vote /vout/ *v.* to show by marking a paper, raising your hand, etc. which person you want to elect or whether you support a particular plan: *Greg says he has never voted.* | *Who did you vote for in the last election?*

SOURCE: *Longman Advanced American Dictionary*

B DISCUSSION. Should every country have the same form of government? Why don't all countries have the same form of government? In your opinion, which is the best form of government?

C SOUND BITES. Read along silently as you listen to a conversation in the United States.

SAN-CHI: So what are you up to these days, Sam?
SAM: Hi, San-Chi! What a coincidence. I've been meaning to give you a call. I need some cultural advice.
SAN-CHI: What about?
SAM: Well, I'm having dinner at Mei-Li's house tonight, and her parents are in from Taiwan.
SAN-CHI: Really?
SAM: Mm-hmm. And you know how much I love to talk politics. Would it be rude to bring that up at the dinner table?
SAN-CHI: Uh … Well, not really. Most people from Taiwan like to talk about politics too. But it would not be cool to argue with them if you don't agree with what they say!
SAM: How well you know me! I do tend to be a little opinionated.
SAN-CHI: Well, in that case, I'd advise you to talk about something else!

D IN OTHER WORDS. Find a word or expression in the conversation that is similar in meaning to each of the following words and expressions.

1. What have you been doing lately?
2. Yes.
3. Would it be impolite to talk about that?
4. It wouldn't be OK.
5. I express my beliefs strongly.

WHAT ABOUT YOU?

How much do you know about governments around the world? Write the names of countries on the chart. Then compare your chart with your classmates' charts.

a democracy	a monarchy	a dictatorship

DISCUSSION. **Do you like to talk about politics? Do you think politics is a good topic for discussion when you are invited to someone's home?**

LESSON

1 Ask If It's OK to Discuss a Topic

CONVERSATION MODEL Read and listen.

A: In general, is it acceptable here to ask people about politics?
B: That depends. If you know someone well, it's OK.
A: Well, would it be OK to ask you?
B: Sure! What would you like to know?
A: Who do you think will win the election?
B: That's a good question!

Rhythm and intonation practice

VOCABULARY. A continuum of political and social beliefs. Listen and practice.

radical *adj.* supporting complete political or social change —**a radical** *n.*

liberal *adj.* supporting changes in political, social, or religious systems that allow more people to do what they want —**a liberal** *n.*

moderate *adj.* having opinions or beliefs, especially about politics, that are not extreme and that most people consider reasonable or sensible —**a moderate** *n.*

conservative *adj.* preferring to continue to do things as they have been done in the past rather than risking changes —**a conservative** *n.*

reactionary *adj.* strongly opposed to political or social change —**a reactionary** *n.*

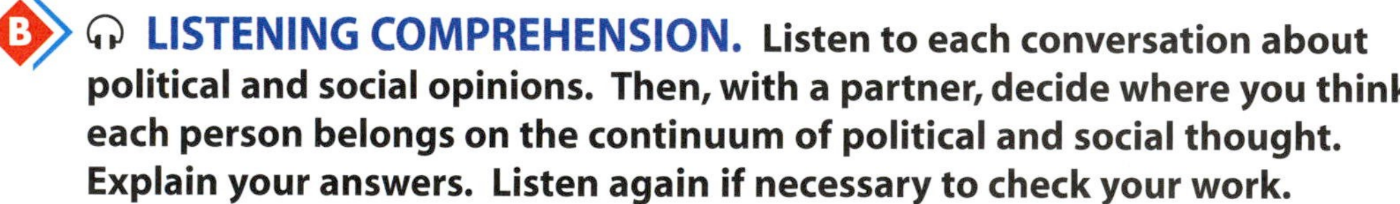

B LISTENING COMPREHENSION. Listen to each conversation about political and social opinions. Then, with a partner, decide where you think each person belongs on the continuum of political and social thought. Explain your answers. Listen again if necessary to check your work.

Conversation	radical	liberal	moderate	conservative	reactionary
1. He's					
2. She's					
3. He's					
4. She's					
5. He's					

GRAMMAR. Non-count nouns for abstract ideas

Nouns that represent abstract ideas are non-count nouns.

Remember: non-count nouns are neither singular nor plural. They have no plural form, and they are not preceded by the, a, or an. When a non-count noun is the subject of a sentence, use a singular verb.

Education is an important issue.
NOT ~~The~~ education is an important issue. NOT ~~Educations are~~ an important issue.

Nouns for abstract ideas

advice	information	progress
education	justice	proof
health	news	time
help	peace	work
importance	poverty	

PAGE G15
For more ...

D Complete each statement with the correct form of the nouns and verbs.

1. Our ________ (advice / advices) to you ______ (is / are) to avoid discussing politics.
2. ________ (Poverty / The poverty) ______ (was / were) the topic of the international conference.
3. Both candidates have programs for ________ (the health / health) and ________ (educations / education).
4. There is no ________ (proof / proofs) they've made ________ (a progress / progress) in fighting ________ (injustice / the injustice).
5. Making ________ (peace / the peace) takes a lot of ________ (works / work) and a long time.
6. Good news ________ (is / are) hard to find in the newspaper these days.

E PRONUNCIATION. Stress to emphasize meaning. Listen and practice the different intonations of this sentence.

1. Are you in favor of censorship? (normal stress)
2. **ARE** you in favor of censorship? (I need to know whether you are or you aren't.)
3. Are **YOU** in favor of censorship? (I'm surprised you would have that opinion.)
4. Are you in **FA**vor of censorship? (I thought you were against it.)
5. Are you in favor of **CEN**sorship? (Are you in favor of that?)

Now, with a partner, take turns saying a sentence out loud. Your partner points to the sentence you read and reads the meaning of that stress pattern.

CONVERSATION PAIR WORK

Check the questions that you think are OK to ask someone you don't know well. Compare your answers with a partner's. Do you agree?

- ☐ Are most people here liberal or conservative?
- ☐ Are you liberal or conservative?
- ☐ Who's going to win the election?
- ☐ Who are you voting for?
- ☐ What do you think of the president / prime minister / king / queen?

Now role-play a conversation with someone visiting from another country. Use the conversation model on page 100 as a guide.

LESSON

2 Discuss Controversial Issues Politely

CONVERSATION MODEL Read and listen.

A: Are you in favor of capital punishment?
B: Yes, I am. I believe if you kill someone you deserve to be killed. What about you?
A: Actually, I'm against the death penalty. I think it's wrong to take a life, no matter what.
B: Well, I guess we'll have to agree to disagree!

Rhythm and intonation practice

Disagreement
Really? I have to disagree with you there.
Do you think so? I'm not sure I agree.
Well, I'm afraid I don't agree.

Agreement
I agree with you on that one.
I couldn't agree more.
I couldn't have said it better myself.
That's exactly what I think.

VOCABULARY. Some controversial issues. Listen and practice.

censorship of books and movies

compulsory military service

lowering the driving age

raising the voting age

prohibiting smoking indoors

your own controversial issue: ______________________

LISTENING COMPREHENSION. Listen to people's opinions about controversial issues. Then listen again and complete each statement with <u>for</u> or <u>against</u>.

1. She's ________ prohibiting smoking indoors.
2. He's ________ compulsory military service.
3. She's ________ raising the driving age.
4. He's ________ lowering the voting age.
5. She's ________ censorship of TV programs.

C DISCUSSION. Which of the people's opinions do you agree or disagree with? Give reasons.

D GRAMMAR. Verbs followed by objects and infinitives

Certain verbs can be followed by infinitives, but some verbs must be followed by an object before the infinitive.

The newspaper reminded **all 18-year-olds** to vote.

We urged **them** to write letters against the death penalty.

The law requires **everyone** to wear a seatbelt.

Verbs followed directly by an infinitive

agree	decide	manage	pretend
appear	deserve	need	refuse
can't afford	hope	offer	seem
can't wait	learn	plan	

Verbs followed by an object before an infinitive

advise	convince	permit	request	urge
allow	encourage	persuade	require	warn
cause	invite	remind	tell	

More complete lists can be found on page 130.

PAGE G16
For more ...

E PAIR WORK. Using an object before the infinitive, change each sentence from the passive voice to the active voice. Use the phrase in parentheses as the subject of the sentence.

"The teachers **persuaded the school administration to vote** against the new rules."

1. The school administration was persuaded (by the teachers) to vote against the new rules.
2. We were reminded (by our friends) to vote early.
3. I was invited (by the town) to give a speech about violence in movies.
4. The voters were convinced (by accident statistics) to change the driving age.
5. Citizens are expected (by the government) to register for military service at age 18.
6. People are not permitted (by the city) to smoke in public buildings.

CONVERSATION PAIR WORK

Express your opinion about a controversial issue. Agree or disagree politely. Use these issues or another controversial issue you have an opinion about.
Start like this:

A: Are you in favor of _____?

B: _____ ...

Continue the conversation in your <u>own</u> way.

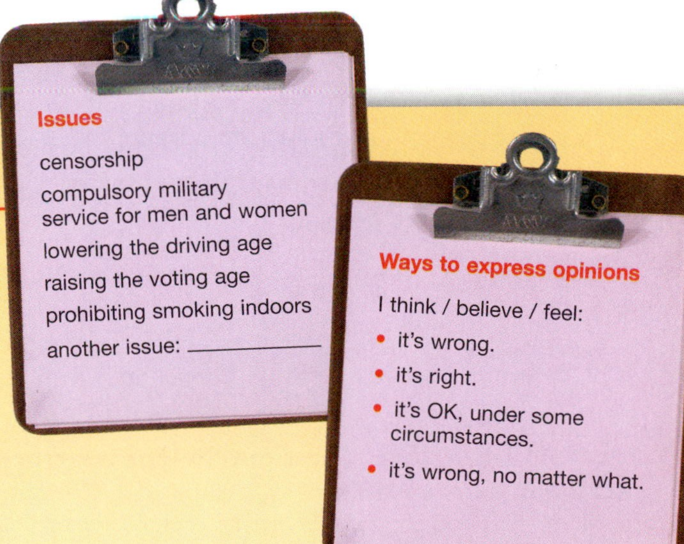

Issues
censorship
compulsory military service for men and women
lowering the driving age
raising the voting age
prohibiting smoking indoors
another issue: _____
Ways to express opinions
I think / believe / feel:
• it's wrong.
• it's right.
• it's OK, under some circumstances.
• it's wrong, no matter what.

LESSON 3

Propose Solutions to Global Problems

 **READING WARM-UP.** **What do you think are the most serious problems in the world today?**

 **READING.** **Read about some issues people are talking about. Are these problems growing or decreasing in the world today?**

The following issues were most frequently mentioned in a global survey about current world problems.

Poverty

Approximately one-fifth of the world's population, over one billion people, earns less than US$ 1.00 a day. Each day, over a billion people in the world lack basic food supplies. And each day, 35,000 children under the age of five die of starvation or preventable infectious disease.

Corruption

People all over the world complain about the corruption of police, government officials, and business leaders. Three examples of corruption are:

- a police officer takes money [a bribe] from a driver so he doesn't give the driver a ticket for speeding
- a public official gives a government contract to a company in which he or she has a financial interest
- a company that wants to do business with a government agency offers a public official money or a gift to choose that company for the job

Some people feel that power promotes corruption and that corruption is just an unavoidable part of human nature. But everyone agrees that it is a terrible problem all over the world.

Terrorism

Every day we see or hear about terrorism and terrible violent acts committed against innocent people for religious or political reasons. Many ask why terrorism is on the rise.

Some social scientists believe that television and movies may contribute to growing anger. They claim that some people may feel frustrated and powerless when they measure their lives against the lives of extremely wealthy people they see in the media.

Racism and ethnic discrimination

Racism and ethnic discrimination exist in many places. These two terrible problems cause human rights violations all over the world. But what causes racism and ethnic discrimination?

At the core, both result from the belief that genetic or cultural differences produce the superiority or inferiority of one group over another. When taken to the extreme, some racists justify the domination and destruction of groups they consider to be either superior or inferior. Although we like to believe that humans have progressed away from such discredited ideas, the history of the last hundred years has seen some of the worst examples of racism and ethnic discrimination in history: the European Holocaust, South African apartheid, and massacres in Eastern Europe and the Sudan are only a few of the tragic events of recent times.

C UNDERSTANDING FROM CONTEXT. **Based on the reading, write the problems described by the following statements.**

1. lack of necessary money to survive: ______________
2. judging or harming people because of their genetic heritage: ______________
3. abuse of power by people in government or business: ______________
4. extreme violence toward innocent victims: ______________

D CLASSIFICATION. **Cross out the one word or phrase that is unrelated to the others. Explain your reasoning.**

1.	people	politics	ethnic groups	races
2.	money	property	income	racism
3.	bribe	corruption	discrimination	money
4.	hunger	starvation	domination	lack of food
5.	racism	business	discrimination	prejudice

TOP NOTCH INTERACTION • *Repairing the world*

STEP 1. Which world issues concern you the most? Put this list in order of importance for you, from 1 to 6, with 1 being the most important. Then rank them in order of difficulty to accomplish from 1 to 6, with 1 being the most difficult.

Order of importance		Order of difficulty to accomplish
◯	reducing poverty and hunger	◯
◯	preventing terrorism	◯
◯	avoiding war	◯
◯	ending or reducing corruption	◯
◯	wiping out racism and ethnic discrimination	◯
◯	protecting human rights	◯

STEP 2. PAIR WORK. On your notepads, write some approaches you think would be effective for each problem. If you know a place that has that problem, write the name of the place.

problem	place	possible approaches
reducing hunger/poverty	Haiti	collect packages of food to send

problem	place	possible approaches

STEP 3. DISCUSSION. Discuss world or local problems with your classmates. Do you all have the same concerns? Do you agree on the solutions?

STEP 4. WRITING. Write about one of the problems you discussed. In the first paragraph, identify the problem. Talk about the place, giving as many details as you can. In the second paragraph, write about the solution. Use your notepad and your discussion notes for support.

LESSON

4 Debate the Pros and Cons of Issues

A VOCABULARY. **Ways to disagree politely.** **Listen and practice.**

1. "I think smoking is a disgusting habit."
   "**That may be true, but** if you only smoke in your own house, you're not hurting anyone but yourself."

2. "I think more people should be active in politics. That way we would have better governments."
   "**I see what you mean, but** it's not realistic to expect everyone to care."

3. "Our president is doing an excellent job."
   "**Well, on the one hand,** he's not corrupt. **But on the other hand,** he hasn't done much to improve the country."

4. "I think we should just vote against everyone who's in office now. That's a good way to get change."
   "**That's one way to look at it, but** how do we know inexperienced candidates will be any better than what we already have?"

B PAIR WORK. **Take turns saying and responding to each opinion below. Use the phrases in the vocabulary above and the expressions from page 102 to agree or disagree.**

1. "Actually, in some countries, dictatorship has helped stop corruption."
   "I couldn't agree with you more. Countries with dictatorships are better off." **OR** "That may be true, but no one should have to live under a dictatorship."
2. "There is no real democracy. All governments are controlled by a few powerful people."
3. "I think moderates are the only people you can trust in government."
4. "I'm not going to vote. All the candidates are corrupt."

C LISTENING COMPREHENSION. **Listen to three conversations about politics. Then listen again and work in pairs. Partner A: Summarize the argument in favor. Partner B: Summarize the argument against.**

1. **about dictatorship**
   Partner A (pro): ____________________
   Partner B (con): ____________________
2. **about democracy**
   Partner A (pro): ____________________
   Partner B (con): ____________________
3. **about monarchy**
   Partner A (pro): ____________________
   Partner B (con): ____________________

TOP NOTCH
INTERACTION • *That's one way to look at it!*

STEP 1. **As a class, choose an issue that you'd like to debate.**

Democracy

Capital Punishment

Censorship

Your own local political issue: ______

STEP 2. **PAIR WORK.** **On your notepads, write arguments for and against.**

arguments in favor:

arguments against:

STEP 3. **DEBATE.** **Divide the class in half, with one side in favor and the other side against. Take turns presenting your views. Sit or stand with the people who have the same argument as you. Take turns and disagree politely.**

NEED HELP? **Here's language you already know:**

Discuss controversies politely

Are you in favor of ___?
That's a good question!
It's not cool to ___.
I tend to be a little opinionated.
I'm opposed to ___ / in favor of ___.
I think / believe / feel
- it's wrong.
- it's right.
- it's OK under some circumstances.
- it's wrong no matter what.

Express agreement

I agree with you on that one.
I couldn't agree more.
I couldn't have said it better myself.
That's exactly what I think.

Express disagreement

We'll have to agree to disagree!
I have to disagree with you there.
I'm not sure I agree.
I'm afraid I don't agree.

UNIT 9
CHECKPOINT

A **LISTENING COMPREHENSION. Listen to the excerpts from a radio news program. Write the four problems being reported.**

1. ______________________
2. ______________________
3. ______________________
4. ______________________

B **Using an object before the infinitive, change each sentence from the passive voice to the active voice. Use the phrase in parentheses as the subject of the sentence.**

1. The president is not allowed (by the law) to change the Constitution.
   The law doesn't allow the president to change the Constitution.
2. Presidents are required (by the Constitution) to leave office after two terms.
   ____
3. The candidates were invited (by the election committee) to speak about their policies.
   ____
4. We were advised (by all our friends) not to be disappointed about the election.
   ____

C **Complete the paragraph about an election.**

Many ________ (1. candidate / candidates) running for election make ________ (2. promise / promises) about ________ (3. education / the education). But ________ (4. progress / the progress) comes slowly, and ________ (5. information / informations) ________ (6. is / are) hard to get. Voters would like to see ________ (7. proof / the proof) that their ________ (8. advice / advices) ________ (9. is /are) being followed. For instance, we are just now receiving ________ (10. the news / news) of education statistics and ________ (11. it's / they're) not very good. ________ (12. Help / The help) is needed, and ________ (13. the time / time) is necessary to improve our schools.

D **WRITING. Write about one of the following issues: compulsory military service, capital punishment, censorship of books and movies. Include both the pros and cons of the issue.**

***TOP NOTCH* PROJECT**
Find articles in the newspaper about world problems. Describe the problem and suggest solutions. Post your solutions on a bulletin board.

***TOP NOTCH* WEBSITE**
For Unit 9 online activities, visit the *Top Notch* Companion Website at www.longman.com/topnotch.

UNIT WRAP-UP

- **Vocabulary.** What do you think the people are talking about in each conversation?
- **Social Language.** Role-play polite political discussions for the people. Agree and disagree.

Now I can ...

- ☐ ask if it's OK to discuss a topic.
- ☐ discuss controversial issues politely.
- ☐ propose solutions to global problems.
- ☐ debate the pros and cons of issues.

UNIT 10

Enjoying the World

UNIT GOALS

1 Warn about a possible risk
2 Describe where a place is located
3 Describe a natural setting
4 Debate about development

 **TOPIC PREVIEW.** Are you good at reading maps? Study the map.

COSTA RICA

CENTRAL AMERICA
COSTA RICA
Lake Nicaragua
NICARAGUA
Lake Arenal
Arenal Volcano
Liberia
La Fortuna
Caribbean Sea
COSTA RICA
Puntarenas
San José
Irazu Volcano
Puerto Limón
N
W
E
S
Gulf of Nicoya
Pacific Ocean
Quepos
Coronado Bay
PANAMA
Gulf of Dulce

Mountain Ranges
1 Guanacaste Range
2 Central Volcanic Range
3 Talamanca Range
▲ = Volcano
● = City
★ = Capital City

National Parks
4 La Amistad
5 Chirripó
6 Corcovado
7 Braulio Carrillo
8 Santa Rosa
9 Tortuguero

0 50 100 kilometers
0 31 62 miles

 **Use the map to answer the questions about Costa Rica.**

1. What's the capital city?
2. What two bodies of water are on either coast of Costa Rica?
3. What two countries share a border with Costa Rica?
4. What's the largest national park?
5. What's the largest lake in Costa Rica?
6. Approximately how far is Puntarenas from San José?
7. In which mountain range is San José located?

C **SOUND BITES.** **Read along silently as you listen to a conversation in Costa Rica between Carlo, from Italy, and David, from Hong Kong.**

CARLO: You wouldn't happen to know anything about the waterfall at La Fortuna, would you? We've been planning to rent a car and drive up there this weekend.

DAVID: Actually, we just got back from there yesterday.

CARLO: What a coincidence! Is it worth seeing?

DAVID: You definitely don't want to miss it. The whole setting is really breathtaking.

CARLO: Good. I can't wait.

DAVID: But watch out on your way down. The path can get pretty wet, so be sure to take it slow.

CARLO: Thanks for the warning. What if we want to get a look at the Arenal Volcano, too? Do you think that's all doable in two days?

DAVID: It's only about twenty minutes west of La Fortuna. I'm sure you could handle both.

La Fortuna waterfall

D **IN OTHER WORDS.** **Read the conversation again and restate the following underlined words and phrases in your own way.**

1. "Is it worth seeing?"
2. "The whole setting is really breathtaking."
3. "But watch out on your way down."
4. "Be sure to take it slow."
5. "What if we want to get a look at the Arenal Volcano, too?"
6. "Do you think that's all doable in two days?"
7. "I'm sure you could handle both."

WHAT ABOUT **YOU?**

Write the name of places you know for each of the following geographical features.

an ocean or a sea:	a lake:
a bay or gulf:	a mountain or volcano:
a mountain range:	a capital city:
a national park:	

LESSON

1 Warn about a Possible Risk

CONVERSATION MODEL Read and listen.

A: Excuse me. Can you tell me the way to the beach?
B: That way. It's not very far.
A: Thanks. Do you think the water's too cold to go swimming?
B: Not at all. But you should be careful. The undertow can be quite dangerous.
A: Thanks for the warning.

undertow

Rhythm and intonation practice

A VOCABULARY. Describe possible risks. Listen and practice.

It can be quite **dangerous**.

It can be very **rocky**.

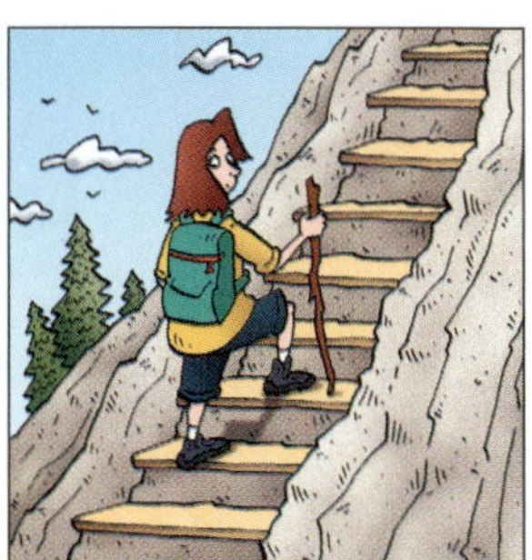
It can be extremely **steep**.

It can be really **foggy**.

It can be quite **slippery**.

It can be pretty **dark**.

It can be terribly **exhausting**.

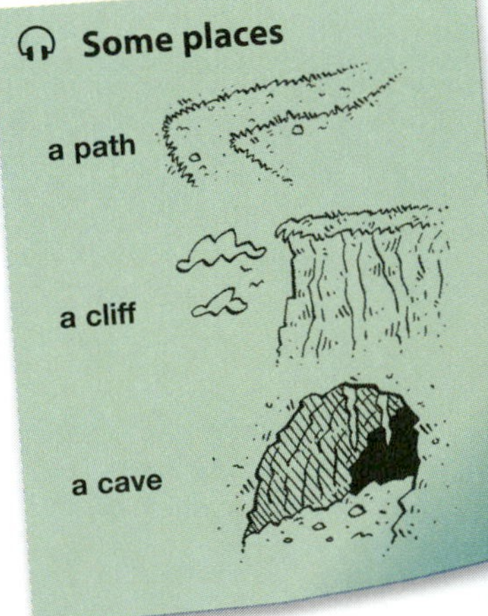

B LISTENING COMPREHENSION. Listen to the conversations.

Check if the speaker thinks the place is safe or dangerous.

	is completely safe.	could be dangerous.
1. She thinks that swimming in the bay …	☐	☐
2. He thinks that hiking around the waterfall …	☐	☐
3. She thinks climbing the mountain …	☐	☐
4. He thinks swimming in the river …	☐	☐

C GRAMMAR. Infinitives with too

Use an infinitive after too and an adjective to give a warning or an explanation.

It's **too dangerous to go** swimming at that beach. = Don't go swimming there because it's dangerous.
It's **too dark to go** hiking. = Don't go hiking now because it's too dark.
Those cliffs are **too steep to climb**. = Don't climb them because they're very steep.

You can clarify with a for phrase.

Those cliffs are too steep **for you** to climb.
It's too dangerous **for children** to go swimming at that beach.

BE CAREFUL!
Don't say:
Those cliffs are too steep to climb ~~them~~.

PAGES G16–G17
For more ...

D Write sentences using too + an infinitive and a for phrase.

1. It's ______________ to that neighborhood alone.
   dangerous / you / go
2. This map of the national park is ______________.
   confusing / me / understand
3. The ancient monuments you want to see aren't ______________.
   steep / you / climb
4. It's not ______________ the 6:00 train to the capital.
   late / you / catch
5. The path is ______________ on safely.
   rocky / your children / walk
6. It's really ______________ to the waterfall today.
   hot / us / go hiking

CONVERSATION PAIR WORK

Role-play asking for directions to a place. Warn about possible risks or dangerous animals or insects. Use the pictures and the guide, or create a new conversation.

Places to go
the waterfall
the path
the cave
the beach
the cliffs

A: Excuse me. Can you tell me the way to ____?
B: ____ .
A: Thanks.
B: But you should be careful. The ____ can be quite ____ .
A: ____ ...

a scorpion

a jellyfish

a mosquito

a snake

a shark

CONTROLLED PRACTICE

LESSON 2

Describe Where a Place is Located

CONVERSATION MODEL Read and listen.

A Where exactly is Miyajima Island located?

B: About an hour west of Osaka by train. Are you planning on going?

A: I've been thinking about it.

B: It's a must-see. Be sure to take pictures!

Rhythm and intonation practice

Positive comments
It's a must-see.
You don't want to miss it.

Negative comments
It's overrated.
It's a waste of time.

GRAMMAR. Prepositions of place

Cobán is **in** the central part **of** Guatemala.

Tikal is **in** the North.

Belize is northeast **of** Guatemala.

Quetzaltenango is about 100 kilometers west **of** Guatemala City.

Champerico is **on** the west coast **of** Guatemala.

Flores is **on** the south shore **of** Lake Petén Itzá.

El Rancho is located **on** the Motagua River.

PAGES G17–G19
For more ...

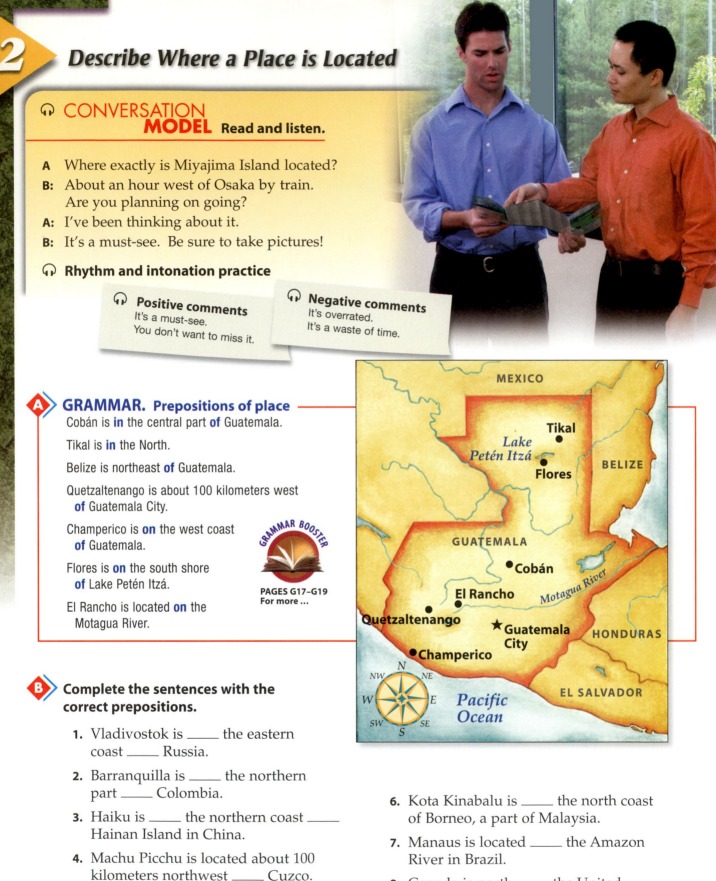

B Complete the sentences with the correct prepositions.

1. Vladivostok is _____ the eastern coast _____ Russia.
2. Barranquilla is _____ the northern part _____ Colombia.
3. Haiku is _____ the northern coast _____ Hainan Island in China.
4. Machu Picchu is located about 100 kilometers northwest _____ Cuzco.
5. Vietnam is south _____ China.
6. Kota Kinabalu is _____ the north coast of Borneo, a part of Malaysia.
7. Manaus is located _____ the Amazon River in Brazil.
8. Canada is north _____ the United States.

C PRONUNCIATION. Voiced and voiceless th. Listen and repeat.

voiceless th	voiced th
1. north	5. the West
2. northeastern	6. this way
3. south	7. northern
4. southwestern	8. southern

Now listen to the words. Check if the th is voiceless or voiced.

	voiceless th	voiced th
1. thanks	☐	☐
2. breathtaking	☐	☐
3. though	☐	☐
4. path	☐	☐
5. breathe	☐	☐

Miyajima Island, Japan

CONVERSATION PAIR WORK

Role-play a conversation about the location of an interesting place. Use the maps or your own map. Start like this:

A: Where exactly is _____ located?

B: _____ . . .

Continue the conversation in your own way.

LESSON 3

Describe a Natural Setting

Positive adjectives to describe the beauty of nature

The scenery was **breathtaking**.
The views were **spectacular**.
The sights were **extraordinary**.

A VOCABULARY. Describing the natural world.

Listen and practice.

GEOGRAPHIC ADJECTIVES

mountainous

hilly

flat

lush

arid

GEOGRAPHIC NOUNS

a forest

a jungle

a canyon

an island

a valley

B LISTENING COMPREHENSION.

Listen to Kenji Ozaki describe a trip he took several years ago. Check the natural features he saw.

- ☐ super-high waterfall
- ☐ super-high cliffs
- ☐ an ancient valley
- ☐ an ancient forest
- ☐ extraordinary trees
- ☐ extraordinary jungles
- ☐ fresh water
- ☐ fresh air

SOURCE: Authentic *Top Notch* interview

Kenji Ozaki
Tokyo, Japan

Listen again. Answer the questions.

1. What country did Kenji Ozaki visit?
2. What kind of a place did he visit?
3. What do you think he liked best about it? Why?

STEP 1. **On your notepad, write about a spectacular place. Write about a place you've visited or research the places in the pictures. What does it look like? What can you do there?**

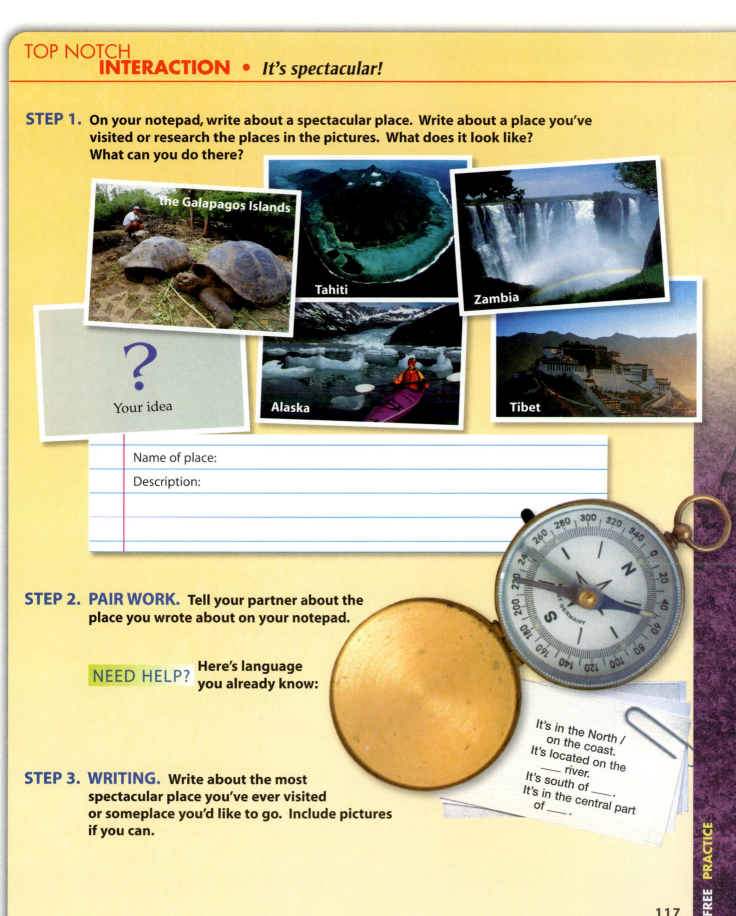

Name of place:

Description:

STEP 2. **PAIR WORK.** **Tell your partner about the place you wrote about on your notepad.**

NEED HELP? **Here's language you already know:**

It's in the North / on the coast.
It's located on the ___ river.
It's south of ___.
It's in the central part of ___.

STEP 3. **WRITING.** **Write about the most spectacular place you've ever visited or someplace you'd like to go. Include pictures if you can.**

Debate the Pros and Cons of Development

LESSON

A READING WARM-UP. **Are there any places in the world where you think tourism would be a danger to the environment? Why?**

B READING. **Read the article. Does ecotourism sound like an interesting way to take a vacation? Why or why not?**

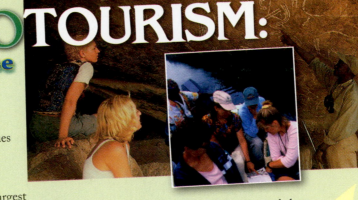

ECOTOURISM: the Promise and Perils

Worldwide, tourism generates annual revenues of nearly 3 trillion US dollars—nearly 11% of all global revenues—making it the world's largest industry. In recent years, ecotourism—or environmentally friendly tourism—has grown in popularity, uniting the interests of both environmentalists and developers. However, finding a compromise between the environment and development is often challenging, and ecotourism can actually cause additional problems for the very regions it is supposed to protect.

Practically speaking, ecotourism includes activities in which visitors enjoy hands-on experiences, such as bird-watching in the Brazilian rainforest, hiking in the mountains of Nepal, participating in a traditional village celebration, or taking a canoe trip down a river. Local guides usually accompany small groups of tourists, teaching them all about local plants and animals and the culture of the region. Tourists typically stay with local families, or at small, environmentally friendly hotels. The cross-cultural exchange that is part of the experience adds greatly to its value for many people. Ecotourism also encourages the development of native handicrafts and artwork for souvenirs, and thus contributes to the preservation of cultural heritage.

Ecotourism presents an alternative to traditional approaches to economic development, such as farming, logging, mining, or hunting. It offers local people the chance to escape a cycle of poverty and, by sharing their knowledge of the local terrain and ecology with visitors, to develop a stronger sense of community pride.

However, ecotourism is not always beneficial to local people and the ecology. Any increase in population, however temporary, produces larger amounts of waste and pollution and can require more development. Tourist overcrowding is causing severe environmental damage to the Galapagos Islands, for example. Tourists who go to view wildlife can scare animals away from their feeding and nesting sites. Tourism may even encourage the development of markets in wildlife souvenirs (skins, bones, etc.) which further damages the environment.

Farming, mining, logging, and hunting are traditional approaches to economic development.

Glossary

the environment the air, water, and land in which people, animals, and plants live

ecology the way in which plants, animals, and people are related to each other and to their environment

development planning and building new houses, streets, etc. on land

SOURCE: Cambridge Scientific Abstracts (*Hot Topics* series), www.csc.com

C PAIR WORK. **Find these expressions in the article. Explain what they mean.**

1. environmentally friendly
2. cross-cultural exchange
3. preservation of cultural heritage
4. environmental damage

DISCUSSION.

1. Do you think the article makes a stronger argument for or against ecotourism?
2. Why do you think ecotourism has become so popular in recent years?

TOP NOTCH INTERACTION • *That's one way to look at it…*

STEP 1. GROUP WORK. Divide the class into groups of developers and groups of environmentalists. Decide what can be done to develop Miquelon's economy while protecting its beautiful environment.

Developers:
You want to develop the economy.

Environmentalists:
You want to protect the environment.

Miquelon

The fishing village of Miquelon is "off the beaten path"— on a rocky but very scenic island with little tourism and no industry to speak of.

Population: 1,000
Location: Off the coast of Newfoundland, Canada
Language: French
Food: Excellent authentic French cuisine!

Attractions:
- a small fishing village with colorful houses and friendly people
- a bay where thousands of seals come to give birth to baby seals
- beautiful beaches, good for swimming in summer. Low forests, good for hunting
- hiking: spectacular views of the ocean and cliffs, beautiful wildflowers, wild horses
- interesting history
- whale-watching: breathtaking views of whales in their natural habitat

Problems:
- small population and no real hotels (But foreign students have stayed in homes to learn French.)
- pollution: garbage thrown off a cliff on the western coast
- no industry or farming, no tall trees for logging
- decline in fishing jobs: too much fishing led to a decline in fish

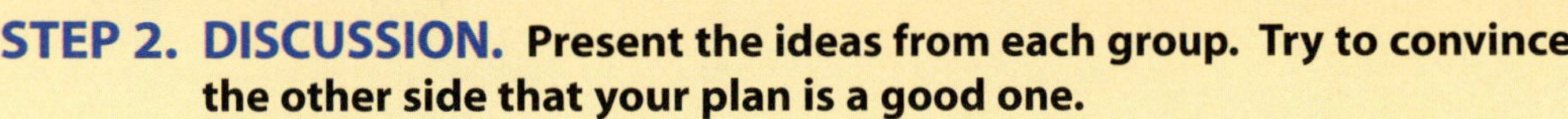

STEP 2. DISCUSSION. Present the ideas from each group. Try to convince the other side that your plan is a good one.

NEED HELP? Here's language you already know:

Are you in favor of ____ ? I think it's wrong to ____ . I think it's a good idea to ____ . I'm against ____ .	It isn't acceptable to ____ . That's true, but ____ . I see what you mean, but ____ .	On the one hand, ____ . But on the other hand, ____ . That's one way to look at it, but ____ . That depends.

FREE PRACTICE

UNIT **10**
CHECKPOINT

A **LISTENING COMPREHENSION.** **Listen to the conversations. Check the type of place each person is talking about. Check whether or not the person recommends going there.**

	type of place?			recommends going?	
1.	☐ a canyon	☐ a waterfall	☐ cliffs	☐ yes	☐ no
2.	☐ a cave	☐ a canyon	☐ a waterfall	☐ yes	☐ no
3.	☐ a volcano	☐ an island	☐ a canyon	☐ yes	☐ no
4.	☐ a volcano	☐ a valley	☐ a canyon	☐ yes	☐ no

B **Look at the pictures. Complete the warnings about each danger, using too.**

1. 
2. 
3. 
4. 

1. ____________ go swimming in the bay.
2. Those steps ____________ climb.
3. ____________ go in the cave without a flashlight.
4. That road ____________ for us to use.

C **Write the exact locations of the following places. Use the map.**

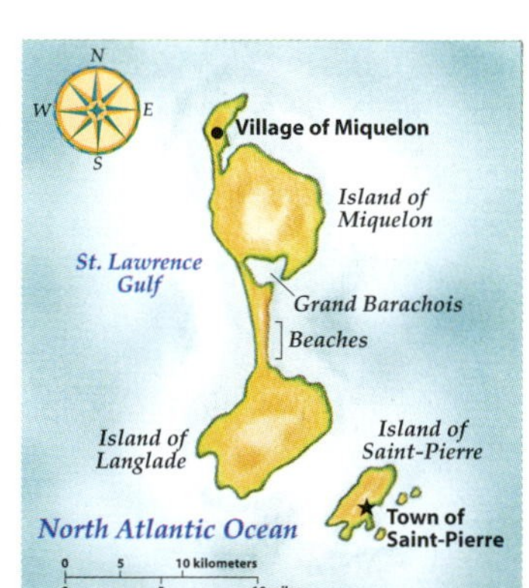

1. The village of Miquelon __is on__ the island of Miquelon.
2. The island of Langlade ____________ the island of Miquelon.
3. The island of Saint-Pierre ____________ Langlade.
4. The village of Miquelon ____________ about ____________ from the town of Saint-Pierre.
5. The beaches ____________ the ____________ coast.

TOP NOTCH PROJECT
Use the Internet to get information about the places in STEP 1 on page 117. Tell your classmates why they should go there.

D **WRITING.** **Write about a natural setting you would like to visit. Say as much as you can. OR Write about your plan for Miquelon. Explain the problem and suggest solutions.**

TOP NOTCH WEBSITE
For Unit 10 online activities, visit the *Top Notch* Companion Website at www.longman.com/topnotch.

Welcome to Honi Honi Island

UNIT WRAP-UP

- **Vocabulary.** Name all the natural and geographical features in the picture.
- **Conversation.** Create conversations for the people on the beach.
- **Grammar.** Write statements warning about risks on the island.
- **Writing.** Write an advertisement to get people to visit Honi Honi Island.

Now I can ...

- ☐ warn about a possible risk.
- ☐ describe where a place is located.
- ☐ describe a natural setting.
- ☐ debate about development.

Alphabetical word list

This is an alphabetical list of all productive vocabulary in the ***Top Notch 3*** units. The numbers refer to the page on which the word first appears or is defined. When a word has two meanings, both are in the list.

Social language list

This is a unit-by-unit list of the productive social language from ***Top Notch 3***.

Unit 1

Allow me to introduce myself.
Everyone calls me [Surat].
Beautiful day, isn't it?
It really is.
By the way, I'm [Jane].

Do you mind my asking you the custom here?
Do you mind if I call you [Rob]?
Would it be rude to call you [Magda]?
Absolutely not.
Please do.

What would you like to be called?
How do you prefer to be addressed?
Do you use Ms. or Mrs.?
You know, you look familiar.

Unit 2

I was wondering if you might be able to recommend [a doctor].
So I hear you're from overseas.
I'm here on business.
Thanks for fitting me in.
This [tooth] is killing me.
Glad to be of help.
I really appreciate it.

Thought I'd better see someone right away.
Well, let's have a look.
I wonder if I might be able to [see the dentist].
Oh, that must hurt.
Are you in a lot of pain?

Well, let me check.
Could you be here by [3:00]?
That would be fine.
You must be [Mr. Brown].
Is anything bothering you today?
Why don't you have a seat?
I'll see if the doctor can see you.

Unit 3

You look like you're in a hurry!
I sure hope so.
But that's not all.
What else?
First thing [Monday morning]
I won't keep you, then.

Do you think I could [get this dry-cleaned by Thursday]?
That might be difficult.
I'm sorry, but it's pretty urgent.
Well, in that case, I'll see what I can do.

I have to get this to [Chicago] a.s.a.p.
Can you recommend a [courier service]?
Why don't you have [Aero Flash] take care of it?
They're really reliable.

Unit 4

I wish I'd [gone to medical school].
Since when have you been [interested in medicine]?
I could have [made a difference].
Maybe it's not too late.
Think so?
Sorry about that.
You can count on me.
Long time no see.
How have you been?

Not bad, thanks.
So what are you doing these days?
No kidding!
How come?
It's hard to make a living [as a painter].
My tastes changed.
My family talked me out of it.
I just changed my mind.
Why do you think that?
Could be. But you never know.

Please tell me something about your [skills].
Do you have knowledge of [Arabic]?
What kind of [talents] do you have?
What [work] experience do you have?
I have experience in [teaching].
I don't have much experience.
I'm good at [math].
I have three years of [French].

Unit 5

[That dress is] spectacular!
What was the occasion?
It takes place [in September].
Oh yeah?
We get together with our [relatives].
[The roads are] impossible.
It takes hours to get anywhere.

I heard there's going to be [a holiday].
What kind of [holiday] is that?
People spend time with their [families].
Have a great [holiday]!
Same to you!
Do you mind if I ask you something?

Of course not.
What's up?
I'm not sure of [the customs here].
Would [flowers] be appropriate?
Absolutely perfect!
It's a good thing I asked.

Unit 6

Oh, my goodness!
What happened?
What a disaster!
That's gigantic!
Any word on [casualties]?
Let's hope for the best.

I wonder if [8.6 is a record].
Believe it or not.
I'm on the line with [your parents].
Would you like to say hello?
I'm running late.
Anything you'd like me to tell them?

There's a storm on its way.
Will do.
What's going on [in the news today]?
What a shame.
Thank goodness [for that].

Unit 7

Looking for anything special?
I'm just browsing.
What are you up to?
I'm picking up [some gardening magazines].
She can't get enough of [them].
Are you reading anything good these days?
Not really.
I just can't seem to get into it.

I guess [poetry] just doesn't turn me on.
I can't put it down.
It's a real page-turner.
Thanks for the tip.
Don't bother.
What's that you're reading?
I've always wanted to read that!
Is it any good?
It's hard to follow.
It's a fast read.

I'd highly recommend it.
Do you mind if I borrow it when you're done?
Not at all.
What incredible [bread]!
I learned how [in the latest issue of Home magazine].
I didn't know they had [recipes].
I'm all thumbs!

Unit 8

[The bugs were] horrendous.
I got eaten alive.
Don't you wish someone would [invent something that works]?
Where have <u>you</u> been?
No way!
I don't believe it.

Do you think I should get the [Brew Rite]?
It's on sale.
That depends.
How much are they selling it for?
Definitely.
That's a great price.
It's top of the line.

Sorry we're late.
We got lost.
That's OK.
It can happen to anyone.
It was entirely my fault.
Better late than never.
Let me get you something to [drink].

Unit 9

So what are you up to these days?
What a coincidence.
I've been meaning to [give you a call].
Would it be rude to [bring that up at the dinner table]?
It would not be cool to [argue with them].
How well you know me!
I do tend to be [a little opinionated].
In general, is it acceptable here to [ask people about politics]?
Would it be OK to [ask you]?

What would you like to know?
That's a good question!
Are you in favor of [capital punishment]?
What about you?
Actually, I'm against [the death penalty].
I think it's wrong to [take a life], no matter what.
I'm opposed to [censorship].
I guess we'll have to agree to disagree.
I have to disagree with you there.
I'm not sure I agree.
I'm afraid I don't agree.

I agree with you on that one.
I couldn't agree more.
I couldn't have said it better myself.
That's exactly what I think.
It's OK, under some circumstances.
That may be true, but ___.
I see what you mean, but ___.
Well, on one hand ___. But on the other hand, ___.
That's one way to look at it.

Unit 10

You wouldn't happen to know anything about [La Fortuna], would you?
Is it worth seeing?
You definitely don't want to miss it.
The whole setting is really [breathtaking].
I can't wait.
Watch out on the way down.
Be sure to take it slow.

Thanks for the warning.
Do you think that's all doable in [two days]?
I'm sure you could handle both.
Can you tell me the way to [the beach].
That way.
Not at all.
[The undertow] can be quite [dangerous].

Where exactly is [Miyajima] located?
About [an hour west of Osaka by train].
Are you planning on going?
I've been thinking about it.
It's a must see.
Be sure to [take pictures]!
You don't want to miss it.
It's overrated.
It's a waste of time.

Pronunciation table

These are the pronunciation symbols used in ***Top Notch 3***.

Vowels

symbol	key word	symbol	key word
i	beat, feed	ə	banana, among
ɪ	bit, did	ɚ	shirt, murder
eɪ	date, paid	aɪ	bite, cry, buy, eye
ɛ	bet, bed	aʊ	about, how
æ	bat, bad	ɔɪ	voice, boy
ɑ	box, odd, father	ɪr	deer
ɔ	bought, dog	ɛr	bare
oʊ	boat, road	ɑr	bar
ʊ	book, good	ɔr	door
u	boot, food, flu	ʊr	tour
ʌ	but, mud, mother		

Consonants

symbol	key word	symbol	key word
p	pack, happy	z	zip, please, goes
b	back, rubber	ʃ	ship, machine, station, special, discussion
t	tie	ʒ	measure, vision
d	die	h	hot, who
k	came, key, quick	m	men
g	game, guest	n	sun, know, pneumonia
tʃ	church, nature, watch	ŋ	sung, ringing
dʒ	judge, general, major	w	wet, white
f	fan, photograph	l	light, long
v	van	r	right, wrong
θ	thing, breath	y	yes
ð	then, breathe	ţ	butter, bottle
s	sip, city, psychology	tˀ	button

Irregular verbs

base form	simple past	past participle
be	was / were	been
become	became	become
begin	began	begun
bite	bit	bit / bitten
bleed	bled	bled
break	broke	broken
bring	brought	brought
build	built	built
burn	burned / burnt	burned / burnt
buy	bought	bought
catch	caught	caught
choose	chose	chosen
come	came	come
cost	cost	cost
cut	cut	cut
do	did	done
draw	drew	drawn
dream	dreamed / dreamt	dreamed / dreamt
drink	drank	drunk
drive	drove	driven
eat	ate	eaten
fall	fell	fallen
feed	fed	fed
feel	felt	felt
fight	fought	fought
find	found	found
fit	fit	fit
flee	fled	fled
fly	flew	flown
forbid	forbade / forbid	forbidden
forget	forgot	forgotten
get	got	gotten
give	gave	given
go	went	gone
grow	grew	grown
have	had	had
hear	heard	heard
hit	hit	hit
hold	held	held
hurt	hurt	hurt
keep	kept	kept
know	knew	known
leave	left	left
lend	lent	lent
let	let	let
lose	lost	lost
make	made	made
mean	meant	meant
meet	met	met
pay	paid	paid
put	put	put
quit	quit	quit
read /rid/	read /rɛd/	read /rɛd/
ride	rode	ridden
ring	rang	rung
rise	rose	risen
run	ran	run
say	said	said
see	saw	seen
sell	sold	sold
send	sent	sent
sew	sewed	sewn
shake	shook	shaken
sing	sang	sung
sit	sat	sat
sleep	slept	slept
speak	spoke	spoken
spend	spent	spent
spread	spread	spread
stand	stood	stood
steal	stole	stolen
stuck	stuck	stuck
sting	stung	stung
strike	struck	struck
swim	swam	swum
take	took	taken
teach	taught	taught
tell	told	told
think	thought	thought
throw	threw	thrown
understand	understood	understood
wake up	woke up	woken up
wear	wore	worn
win	won	won
write	wrote	written

Verb tense review: present, past, and future

THE PRESENT OF BE

Statements

I	am	late.
You We They	are	
He She It	is	

THE SIMPLE PRESENT TENSE

Statements

I You We They	speak English.
He She	speaks English.

Yes / no questions

Do	I you we they	know them?
Does	he she	eat meat?

Short answers

Yes,	I you we they	do.
	he she it	does.

No,	I you we they	don't.
	he she it	doesn't.

Information questions

What do	you we they	need?
When does	he she it	start?
Who	wants needs likes	this book?

THE PRESENT CONTINUOUS

Statements

I	am	watching TV.
You We They	are	studying English.
He She It	is	arriving now.

Yes / no questions

Am	I	going too fast?
Are	you we they	
Is	he she it	

Short answers

Yes,	I	am.
	you	are.
	he she it	is.
	we they	are.

No,	I'm not. you aren't / you're not. he isn't / he's not. she isn't / she's not. it isn't / it's not. we aren't / we're not. they aren't / they're not.

Information questions

What	are	you we they	doing?
When	is	he she it	leaving?
Where	am	I	staying tonight?
Who	is		driving?

THE PAST CONTINUOUS

Statements

I	was	singing that song.
You We They	were	playing the piano.
He She It	was	leaving from Central Station.

Yes / no questions

Was	I he she it	landing in Sydney when the storm began?
Were	we you they	

Short answers

Yes,	I he she it	was.
	we you they	were.

No,	I he she it	wasn't.
	we you they	weren't.

Information questions

When	was	I he she it	speeding?
Where	were	we you they	going?
Who	was		arriving?

THE PAST OF BE

Statements

I He She It	was late.
We You They	were early.

Yes / no questions

Was	I he she it	on time?
Were	we you they	in the same class?

Short answers

Yes,	I he she it	was.
	we you they	were.

No,	I he she it	wasn't.
	we you they	weren't.

Information questions

Where	were	we? you? they?	
When	was	he she it	here?
Who	were	they?	
Who	was	he? she? it?	

THE SIMPLE PAST TENSE

Many verbs are irregular in the simple past tense. See the list of irregular verbs on page 126.

Statements

I You He She It We They	stopped working.

I You He She It We They	didn't start again.

Yes / no questions

Did	I you he she it we they	make a good dinner?

Short answers

Yes,	I you he she it we they	did.

No,	I you he she it we they	didn't.

Information questions

When did	I you he she it we they	read that?
Who		called?

THE FUTURE WITH WILL

Affirmative and negative statements

I You He She It We They	will won't	stop at five o'clock.

Yes / no questions

Will	I you he she it we they	be on time?

Affirmative and negative short answers

Yes,	I you he she it we they	will.
No,		won't.

Information questions

What will	I you he she it we they	do?
Who will		be there?

8 THE FUTURE WITH BE GOING TO

Statements

I'm You're He's She's It's We're They're	going to	be here soon.

I'm You're He's She's It's We're They're	not going to	be here soon.

Yes / no questions

Are	you we they	going to want coffee?
Am	I	going to be late?
Is	he she it	going to arrive on time?

Short answers

Yes,	I	am.
	you	are.
	he she it	is.
	we they	are.

No,	I'm not. you aren't / you're not. he isn't / he's not. she isn't / she's not. it isn't / it's not. we aren't / we're not. they aren't / they're not.

Information questions

What	are	you / we / they	going to see?
When	is	he / she / it	going to shop?
Where	am	I	going to stay tomorrow?
Who	is		going to call?

9 THE PRESENT PERFECT

Affirmative and negative statements

I You We They	have haven't	left yet.
He She It	has hasn't	

Yes / no questions

Have	I you we they	said enough?
Has	he she it	already started?

Affirmative and negative short answers

Yes, No,	I you we they	have. haven't.
Yes, No,	he she it	has. hasn't.

Information questions

Where	have	I you we they	seen that book?
How	has	he she it	been?
Who	has		read it?

10 THE PASSIVE VOICE

Form the passive voice with a form of be and the past participle of the verb

	ACTIVE VOICE	PASSIVE VOICE
simple present	Art collectors **buy** famous paintings.	Famous paintings **are bought by** art collectors.
present continuous	The Cineplex **is showing** that film.	That film **is being shown** by the Cineplex.
present perfect	All the critics **have reviewed** that book.	That book **has been reviewed** by all the critics.
simple past	Vera Wang **designed** this dress.	This dress **was designed** by Vera Wang.
past continuous	Last year, World Air **was** still **selling** tours to the Ivory Coast.	Last year, tours to the Ivory coast **were** still **being sold**.
future with will	The children **will return** the books tomorrow.	The books **will be returned** tomorrow.
be going to	Bart's Garage **is going to repair** my car this afternoon.	My car is **going to be repaired** by Bart's Garage this afternoon.

Verbs followed by a gerund

- acknowledge
- admit
- advise
- appreciate
- avoid
- can't help
- celebrate
- consider
- delay
- deny
- detest
- discontinue
- discuss
- dislike
- endure
- enjoy
- escape
- explain
- feel like
- finish
- forgive
- give up
- imagine
- justify
- keep
- mention
- mind
- miss
- postpone
- practice
- prevent
- prohibit
- propose
- quit
- recall
- recommend
- regret
- report
- resent
- resist
- risk
- suggest
- support
- tolerate
- understand

Verbs followed directly by an infinitive

- afford
- agree
- appear
- arrange
- ask
- attempt
- can't wait
- choose
- consent
- decide
- deserve
- expect
- fail
- grow
- help
- hesitate
- hope
- hurry
- intend
- learn
- manage
- mean
- need
- neglect
- offer
- pay
- plan
- prepare
- pretend
- promise
- refuse
- request
- seem
- struggle
- swear
- volunteer
- wait
- want
- wish
- would like
- yearn

Verbs followed by an object before an infinitive*

- advise
- allow
- ask
- cause
- challenge
- choose
- convince
- enable
- encourage
- expect
- forbid
- force
- get
- help
- hire
- invite
- need
- order
- pay
- permit
- persuade
- promise*
- remind
- request
- require
- teach
- tell
- urge
- want
- warn
- wish
- would like

* These verbs can also be followed by the infinitive without an object (example: *want to speak* or *want someone to speak*).

Verbs followed by either a gerund or an infinitive

- begin
- can't stand
- continue
- forget*
- hate
- like
- love
- prefer
- remember*
- start
- stop*
- try

* There is a big difference in meaning when these verbs are followed by a gerund or an infinitive.

Adjectives followed by an infinitive*

- afraid
- alarmed
- amazed
- angry
- anxious
- ashamed
- curious
- delighted
- depressed
- determined
- disappointed
- distressed
- disturbed
- eager
- easy
- embarrassed
- encouraged
- excited
- fortunate
- glad
- happy
- hesitant
- likely
- lucky
- pleased
- proud
- ready
- relieved
- reluctant
- sad
- shocked
- sorry
- surprised
- touched
- upset
- willing

* EXAMPLE: I'm willing to accept that.

GRAMMAR BOOSTER

The *Grammar Booster* is optional. It provides more explanation and practice, as well as additional grammar concepts.

UNIT 1 Lesson 1

A Correct the error in each item.

1. They'd both like to study abroad, would they?
2. It's only a six-month course, is it?
3. Clark met his wife on a rafting trip, didn't Clark?
4. Marian made three trips to Japan last year, hasn't she?
5. There were a lot of English-speaking people on the tour, wasn't it?
6. The students don't know anything about that, don't they?
7. There isn't any problem with my student visa, isn't there?
8. It's always interesting to travel with people from other countries, aren't they?
9. With English, you can travel to most parts of the world, can you?
10. I'm next, are I?

UNIT 1 Lesson 2

Review: verb usage in the present and past

The simple present tense (and NOT the present continuous)

for facts and regular occurrences

I **study** English. Class **meets** every day. Water **boils** at 100°.

with frequency adverbs and time expressions

They never **eat** before 6:00 on weekdays.

with stative (non-action) verbs

I **remember** her now.

for future actions, especially those indicating schedules

Flight 100 usually **leaves** at 2:00, but tomorrow it leaves at 1:30.

The present continuous (and NOT the simple present tense)

for actions happening now (but NOT with stative verbs)

They**'re talking** on the phone.

for actions occurring during a time period in the present

This year I**'m studying** English.

for some future actions, especially those already planned

Thursday **I'm going** to the theater.

The present perfect or the present perfect continuous

for unfinished or continuous actions

I**'ve lived** here since 2001. OR I**'ve been living** here since 2001.

I**'ve lived** here for five years. OR I**'ve been living** here for five years.

Stative (non-action) verbs

appear	have	own	suppose
be	hear	possess	taste
believe	know	prefer	think
belong	like	remember	understand
contain	look	see	want
cost	love	seem	weigh
feel	need	smell	
hate	notice	sound	

Review: verb usage in the present and past (continued)

The present perfect (but NOT the present perfect continuous)

for completed or non-continuing actions

I've **eaten** there three times.

I've never **read** that book.

I've already **seen** him.

The simple past tense

for actions completed at a specified time in the past

I **ate** there in 2003. NOT ~~I've eaten~~ there in 2003.

The past continuous

for one or more actions in progress at a time in the past

At 7:00, we **were eating** dinner.

They **were swimming** and we **were sitting** on the beach.

The past continuous and the simple past

for an action that interrrupted a continuing action in the past

I **was eating** when my sister **called**.

Used to

for past situations and habits that no longer exist

I **used to smoke**, but I stopped.

They **didn't use to require** a visa, but now they do.

The past perfect

to indicate that one past action preceded another past action

When I arrived, they **had finished** lunch.

A Correct the verbs in the following sentences.

1. I talk on the phone with my fiancé right now.
2. She's usually avoiding sweets.
3. They eat dinner now and can't talk on the phone.
4. Every Friday I'm going to the gym at 7:00.
5. Burt is wanting to go home early.
6. This year we all study English.
7. The train is never leaving before 8:00.
8. Water is freezing when the temperature goes down.
9. We're liking coffee.
10. On most days I'm staying home.

B Complete each sentence with the present perfect continuous.

1. We ______________ (come) to this spa for two years.
2. *Lost in Translation* ______________ (play) at the Classic Cinema since last Saturday.
3. Robert ______________ (wait) for an admissions letter from the language school for a week.
4. The tour operators ______________ (worry about) weather conditions for the rafting trip.
5. I ______________ (talk about) that tour with everyone.

C Check the sentences and questions that express unfinished or continuing actions. Change the verb phrase in those sentences to the present perfect continuous.

☐ **1.** The Averys have lived in New York since the late nineties.
☐ **2.** Their relatives have already called them.
☐ **3.** We have waited to see them for six months.
☐ **4.** I haven't seen the Berlin Philharmonic yet.
☐ **5.** This is the first time I've visited Dubai.
☐ **6.** We have eaten in that old Peruvian restaurant for years.
☐ **7.** Has he ever met your father?
☐ **8.** How long have they studied Arabic?
☐ **9.** My husband still hasn't bought a car.
☐ **10.** The kids have just come back from the race.

D Complete each sentence using the past continuous in one blank and the simple past tense in the other.

1. I ________ (speed) when I ________ (have) the accident.
2. They ________ (watch) TV when they ________ (hear) the news.
3. What ________ (you / do) when I ________ (call)?
4. People ________ (wait) for the theater to open when the fire ________ (start).
5. Who ________ (use) the computer when the electricity ________ (go) off?

UNIT 2 Lesson 1

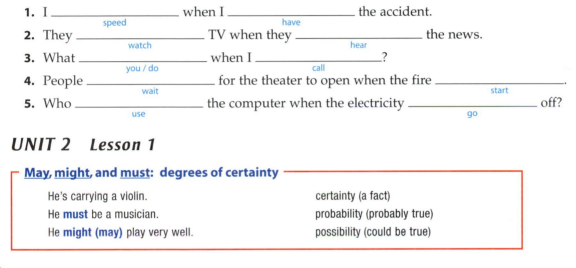

May, might, and must: degrees of certainty

He's carrying a violin.	certainty (a fact)
He **must** be a musician.	probability (probably true)
He **might (may)** play very well.	possibility (could be true)

A Write a statement of certainty, possibility, and probability about the person in each picture.

1. certainty *He's in a lot of pain.*
possibility ________
probability ________

2. certainty ________
possibility ________
probability ________

3. certainty ________
possibility ________
probability ________

UNIT 3 Lesson 1

The passive causative: the by phrase

Use a by phrase if knowing who performed the action is important.

I had my shoes repaired **by a young man** at the train station.

If knowing who performed the action is not important, you don't need to include a by phrase.

I had my shoes repaired ~~by someone~~ at the train station.

Use the cues to write advice about services with the passive causative.

1. shoe / repair / Mr. Gil / Boot Stop *Get your shoes repaired by Mr. Gil at the Boot Stop.*
2. picture / framed / Lydia / Austin Custom Framing ____________
3. hair / cut / Eva / Bella Gente Hair Salon ____________
4. photos / process / mall ____________
5. custom suit / make / Luigi ____________
6. dry cleaning / do/ Midtown Dry Cleaners ____________

UNIT 3 Lesson 2

Complete each sentence with an infinitive, a base form, or a past participle.

1. They got the dry cleaner ____________ (clean) the suit again.
2. He had the photographer ____________ (take) pictures of everyone in the family.
3. I missed class, so I got my classmates ____________ (tell) me what happened that day in class.
4. Are you going to have those pants ____________ (shorten)?
5. She made her son ____________ (stay) in bed because he wasn't feeling well.
6. I'd better get to the bank before it closes if I want to get that check ____________ (cash).
7. Our teacher had us ____________ (write) about what we did during the vacation.
8. You'd better get the travel agent ____________ (change) your flight right away.
9. Are you going to get your paintings ____________ (frame) for the art exhibit?
10. If you need to know when the next train leaves, you can have my assistant ____________ (call) the station.

Let

Use let to show that someone permits someone to do something.

I **don't let** my children **stay** out after 9:00. Why don't you **let** me **help** you?

Let is followed by an object and the base form of a verb.

	object	base form	
She **let**	her sister	**wear**	her skirt.

NOT She let her sister ~~to wear~~ her skirt.

On a separate sheet of paper, rewrite each sentence using let.

1. Don't permit your little brother to open the oven door.
2. You should permit your little sister to go to the store with you.
3. Actually, we don't permit our daughter to eat a lot of candy.
4. I wouldn't permit my youngest son to go to the mall alone.
5. Why won't you permit him to see that movie?
6. You should permit the tailor to do what he thinks is best.
7. We always permit him to stay out late.

Causative have and the past perfect auxiliary have

BE CAREFUL! Don't confuse the simple past tense causative have with have used in the past perfect.

I **had them call** me before 10:00. (They called me.)
I **had called** them before 10:00. (I called them.)

C Who did what? Read the sentence. Complete the statement.

1. We had them fix the car before our trip. ___They___ fixed ___the car___.
   We had fixed the car before our trip. ________ fixed ________.
2. Janet had already called her mother. ________ called ________.
   Janet had her mother call the train station. ________ called ________.
3. Mark had his classmate help him with it. ________ helped ________.
   Mark had helped his classmate with it. ________ helped ________.
4. My father had signed the check for his boss. ________ signed ________.
   My father had his boss sign the check. ________ signed ________.
5. Mr. Gates had them open the bank early. ________ opened ________.
   Mr. Gates had opened the bank early. ________ opened ________.

UNIT 4 Lesson 1

REVIEW: Expressing the future

The future can be expressed in all the following ways:

will + base form	**I'll see**	her tomorrow.
be going to + base form	**I'm going to see**	
the simple present tense	**I see**	
the present continuous	**I'm seeing**	

Modals can also be used to talk about the future.

modal + base form	**I might see**	her tomorrow.
	I may see	
	I can see	

REVIEW: Future with will and be going to

Use will or be going to to make a prediction or to say that something in the future will be true. There is no difference in meaning.

Getting a new car **will cost** a lot of money. Getting a new car **is going to cost** a lot of money.

Use be going to to express a plan.

My tooth has been killing me all week. I'm **going to call** a dentist. NOT ~~I will call~~ a dentist.

Use will for willingness.

A: Is it true you won't go to the dentist?

B: I'**ll go** to the dentist, but I don't like fillings. NOT ~~I'm going to go~~...

A **Complete the conversations using will or be going to.**

1. **A:** Would you like to go running in the park? I ______________ (leave) in about half an hour.

   B: That sounds great. I ______________ (meet) you there.

2. **A:** It's midnight. Why are you still reading?

   B: We ______________ (have) a test tomorrow.

3. **A:** Do you have plans for tomorrow?

   B: Yes. I ______________ (see) a chiropractor for the first time.

4. **A:** I hope you can come tomorrow night. We'd really like you to be there.

   B: OK. I ______________ (come).

5. **A:** I'm thinking about getting a new laptop.

   B: Really? Well, I ______________ (show) you mine. I love it.

REVIEW: The present continuous, the simple present tense, and modals with future meaning

The present continuous

My tooth has been killing me all week. **I'm calling** the dentist tomorrow.

What **are** you **doing** this afternoon? **I'm going** to the beach.

The simple present tense

The office is usually open until 9:00, but it **closes** at 6:00 tomorrow.

Modals should, could, ought to, may, might, have to, and can

You **could** catch the next bus. We **should** call her next week.

B **Read each sentence. Check the sentences that have future meaning.**

- ☐ **1.** Hannah is studying English this month.
- ☐ **2.** Max is studying French next month.
- ☐ **3.** Nancy studies English in the evening.
- ☐ **4.** I'm taking my daughter out for dinner tonight.
- ☐ **5.** You should call me tomorrow.
- ☐ **6.** He might have time to see you later.
- ☐ **7.** My parents are arriving at 10:00.

☐ **8.** The class finishes at 3:00 today.

☐ **9.** The class always starts at 2:00 and finishes at 4:00.

☐ **10.** We may stay another week in Paris.

UNIT 4 Lesson 2

Regrets about the past: wish + the past perfect; should have and ought to have

wish + the past perfect

You can express a regret about the past with wish + the past perfect.

I **wish** I **had married** later. And I **wish** I **hadn't married** Celine!

Do you **wish** you **had bought** that car when it was available?

should have and ought to have

Ought to have has the same meaning as should have. Should have is much more common in spoken English.

I **should have married** later. = I **ought to have married** later.

I **shouldn't have married** Celine. = I **ought not to have** married Celine.

Should he **have married** Celine? = **Ought** he **to have** married Celine?

Note: American English speakers use should have instead of ought to have in negative statements and in questions.

Restate the statements and questions with wish + the past perfect to statements and questions with should have or ought to have.

1. I wish I had studied law. (should) *I should have studied law.*
2. She wishes she had had children. (ought to) ______
3. Do you wish you had studied Chinese? (should) ______
4. I wish I had gone to Chile instead of Australia. (ought to) ______
5. Do you wish you had taken the job at the embassy? (should) ______

UNIT 5 Lesson 1

On a separate sheet of paper, combine the two sentences into one sentence, making the second sentence an adjective clause. Use who or that.

1. The hotel clerk was very helpful. / He recommended the restaurant.
   The hotel clerk who recommended the restaurant was very helpful.
2. My cousin called today. / He lives in New Zealand.
3. We have a meeting every morning. / It begins at 9:30.
4. The celebration is spectacular. / It takes place in spring.
5. The teacher is not very formal. / She teaches the grammar class.
6. Patients might prefer homeopathy. / They want to avoid strong medication.
7. The copy shop is closed on weekends. / It offers express service.
8. The hotel is very expensive. / It has a swimming pool.
9. Do you like the teacher? / He teaches the grammar class.

Reciprocal pronouns: each other and one another

Each other and one another have the same meaning, but one another is more formal.

People give **each other** (or **one another**) gifts. Friends send **each other** (or **one another**) cards.

BE CAREFUL! Reciprocal pronouns have a different meaning from reflexive pronouns.

They looked at **themselves**. (Each person looked in a mirror.)

They looked at **each other**. (Each person looked at the other person.)

On a separate sheet of paper, rewrite each underlined phrase using a reciprocal pronoun.

1. On Christmas, in many places in the world, people give and receive presents.

   On Christmas, in many places in the world, people give each other presents.

2. On New Year's Eve in New York City, people wait in Times Square for midnight to come so they can kiss other people and wish other people a happy new year.
3. During the Thai holiday Songkran, people throw water at other people on the street.
4. During the Tomato Festival in Bunol, Spain, people have a lot of fun throwing tomatoes at other people for about two hours.
5. After a day of fasting during Ramadan, Muslims around the world invite other people to eat in their homes in the evening.

Reflexive pronouns

A reflexive pronoun should always agree with the subject of the verb.

People really enjoy **themselves** during Carnaval.

My sister made **herself** sick from eating so much!

Reflexive pronouns

me → myself
you → yourself
him → himself
her → herself
it → itself
us → ourselves
them → themselves

Common expressions with reflexive pronouns

believe in oneself	If you **believe in yourself**, you can do anything.
enjoy oneself	We **enjoyed ourselves** very much on our vacation.
feel sorry for oneself	Don't sit around **feeling sorry for yourself**.
help oneself to (something)	Please **help yourselves** to dessert!
hurt oneself	Paul **hurt himself** when he tried to move the refrigerator.
give oneself (something)	I wanted to **give myself** a gift, so I bought a watch.
introduce oneself	Why don't you **introduce yourself** to your new neighbor?
be proud of oneself	Jackie **was** really **proud of herself** when she got that job.
take care of oneself	You should **take** better **care of yourself**. OK?
talk to oneself	I sometimes **talk to myself** when I'm feeling nervous.
teach oneself (to do something)	Niki **taught herself** to use a computer.
tell oneself (something)	I always **tell myself** I'm not going to eat dessert, and then I do anyway.
work for oneself	Oscar left the company last year. He now **works for himself**.

Complete the sentences with reflexive pronouns.

1. My brother and his wife really enjoyed ______ on their vacation.
2. My uncle has been teaching ______ how to cook.
3. The food was so terrific that I helped ______ to some more!
4. Don't sit around feeling sorry for ______.
5. I hope your sister's been taking good care of ______.
6. I didn't know anyone at the party, and I was too shy to introduce ______ to anyone.
7. Mr. Yu hurt ______ while lighting firecrackers for the Chinese New Year.

D **Complete each sentence with one of the common expressions with reflexive pronouns.**

1. When did your brother ________________ how to play the guitar?
2. You'd better tell your daughter to stop playing near that stove or she'll ________________.
3. I really hope you ________________ when you're on vacation!
4. To practice greetings and introductions, I ask my students to ________________ to each other on the first day of class.

by + reflexive pronouns

Use by with a reflexive pronoun to mean "alone."

You cannot put on a kimono **by yourself**. You need help.

Students cannot learn to speak in English **by themselves**. They need to practice with each other.

E **Complete each sentence with by and a reflexive pronoun.**

1. Very young children shouldn't be allowed to play outside ________________.
2. Did your father go to the store ________________?
3. When did you learn to fix a computer ________________?
4. We got tired of waiting, so we found a table ________________.

UNIT 5 Lesson 2

Adjective clauses: who and whom in formal English

In formal written or spoken English, use who for subject relative pronouns and whom for object relative pronouns.

The singer was terrible. + **He** sang in the restaurant.

subject relative pronoun

The singer **who** sang in the restaurant was terrible.

The singer was terrible. + We heard **him** last night.

object relative pronoun

The singer **whom** we heard last night was terrible.

A **Complete the sentences with who or whom.**

1. The manager ________________ works at that hotel is very helpful.
2. The man ________________ I met at the meeting has invited us to lunch.
3. The sales representative ________________ lives in Hong Kong may apply for that job.
4. I am very satisfied with the hair stylist ________________ you recommended.
5. The guests ________________ we invited to the event were three hours late.
6. The dentist ________________ you'll see tomorrow speaks English.
7. The DJ ________________ you requested is performing at the club tonight.
8. The tailor ________________ I'm recommending is very reasonable.
9. My friend ________________ works at the embassy will help you.
10. Is your colleague someone ________________ I can really trust?

UNIT 6 Lesson 1

Punctuation rules for direct speech

When writing direct speech, use quotation marks to indicate the words the speaker actually said. Put final punctuation before the second quotation mark.

Jeremy said, "Don't answer the phone."

Use a comma after the verb that introduces the quoted speech.

They said, "Call me after the storm."

Begin the quoted speech with a capital letter.

I said, "Please come to dinner at nine."

On a separate sheet of paper, write and punctuate each of the following statements in direct speech.

1. They said tell us when you will be home *They said, "Tell us when you will be home."*
2. Martin told me don't get a flu shot
3. My daughter said please pick me up after school
4. The English teacher said read the newspaper tonight and bring in a story about the weather
5. We said please don't forget to buy batteries
6. They said don't buy milk
7. We told them please call us in the morning
8. She said please tell your parents I'm sorry I can't talk right now

B Look at each statement in indirect speech. Then complete each statement, making the indirect speech statement a direct speech statement. Use correct punctuation.

1. They told us to be home before midnight. They told us ______
2. The sign downtown said to pack emergency supplies before the storm.
   The sign downtown said ______
3. Your daughter called and told me to turn on the radio and listen to the news about the earthquake. Your daughter told me ______
4. Your parents said not to call them before nine A.M.
   Your parents said ______
5. Mr. Rossi phoned to tell me not to go downtown this afternoon.
   Mr. Rossi told me ______

UNIT 6 Lesson 2

Indirect speech: optional tense changes

When the reporting verbs <u>say</u> or <u>tell</u> are in the simple past tense, it's not always necessary to use a different tense in indirect speech from the one the speaker used. The following are three times when it's optional:

1. **When the statement refers to something JUST said:**
   I just heard the news. They said a storm **is** coming. OR I just heard the news. They said a storm **was** coming.
2. **When the quoted speech refers to something that's still true:**
   May told us she **wants** to get a flu shot tomorrow. OR May told us she **wanted** to get a flu shot tomorrow.
3. **When the quoted speech refers to a scientific or general truth.**
   They said that English **is** an international language. OR They said that English **was** an international language.

BE CAREFUL! Remember that when the reporting verb is in the present tense, the verb tense in indirect speech does not change.

They **say** a big storm **is** expected to arrive tomorrow morning. NOT They say a big storm ~~was~~. . .

On a separate sheet of paper, write each direct speech statement in indirect speech. Change the verb in the indirect speech only if necessary.

1. Last Friday my husband said, "I'm going to pick up some supplies before the storm."
2. Last year my parents said, "We're going to Spain on vacation this year."
3. She told them, "This year's flu shot is not entirely protective against the flu."
4. He just said, "The danger of a flood is over."
5. We always say, "It's always easier to take the train than drive."
6. When I was a child, my parents told me, "It's really important to get a good education."
7. The National Weather Service is saying, "Tonight's weather is terrible."
8. Your parents just told me, "We want to leave for the shelter immediately."

UNIT 7 Lesson 1

Embedded questions: usage

Use embedded questions to ask politely for information.

Can you tell me what time it is?
Could you explain why it's not working?
Do you know where the bathroom is?
Would you mind telling me how to get to Main Street?

Phrases that are often followed by embedded questions:

I don't know...	Can you remember...?
I'd like to know...	Let's ask...
Let me know...	I wonder...
Do you know...?	I'm not sure...
Can you tell me...?	Could you explain...?
I can't remember...	Would you mind telling me...?

BE CAREFUL! Do not use question form in embedded questions.

Do you know **why** she won't read science fiction novels?
NOT Do you know ~~why won't she read science fiction novels~~?

Can you tell me **if** this bus **stops** in Guatemala City?
NOT Can you tell me ~~does this bus stop~~ in Guatemala City?

Embedded questions: punctuation

Sentences with embedded questions are punctuated according to the meaning of the whole sentence.

If an embedded question is in a sentence, end the sentence with a period.

I don't know (something). → I don't know **who she is.**

If an embedded question is in a question, end the question with a question mark.

Can you tell me (something)? → Can you tell me **who she is?**

On a separate sheet of paper, write polite questions using noun clauses with embedded questions. Begin each question differently.

1. You need directions to the airport. *Could you tell me how to get to the airport?*
2. You want to find out what time the concert starts.
3. You don't understand how your new CD player works.
4. You'd like to know why the train is late.
5. You need to find out where the nearest bathroom is.
6. You'd like to know something: Do they speak English at the hotel?

B On a separate sheet of paper, complete each sentence with an embedded question using the question in parentheses. Punctuate each sentence correctly.

1. Please let me know (When does the movie start?)
2. I wonder (Where is the subway station?)
3. Can you tell me (How do you get to King Street?)
4. We're not sure (What should we bring for dinner?)

5. They'd like to understand (Why doesn't Pat want to come to the meeting?)
6. Please tell the class (Who painted this picture?)

C Correct the errors in each item.

1. Could you please tell me ~~does~~ whether this train ~~go~~ goes to Nagoya?
2. I was wondering can I get your phone number?
3. I'd like to know what time does Flight 82 arrive.
4. Can you tell me how much does this magazine cost?
5. Do you remember where did he use to live.
6. I'm not sure why do they keep calling me?
7. I wonder will she come on time?

Embedded questions with infinitives

In embedded questions, an infinitive can be used to express possibility (can or could) or advice (should). You can use an infinitive after the question words when, where, how, who, whom, what, which, or whose.

I don't know where I can get that magazine. = I don't know **where to get** that magazine.
I'm not sure when I should call them. = I'm not sure **when to call** them.
She'd like to know which train she should take. = She'd like to know **which train to take**.

You can use an infinitive after whether.

I don't know whether I should read that book next. = I don't know **whether to read** that book next.

BE CAREFUL! Don't use an infinitive after if.

I'd like to know if I should read that book next. = I'd like to know **whether to read** that book next.
NOT I'd like to know ~~if to read~~ that book next.

D On a separate sheet of paper, rewrite each sentence with an infinitive.

1. Could you tell me whose novel I should read next?
   Could you tell me whose novel to read next?
2. I'd like to know where I can buy Toni Morrison's latest book.
3. Can you remember whom I should call to get that information?
4. I'd like to know which train I can take there.
5. Let me know if I should give her the magazine when I'm done.
6. I wasn't sure when I could get the new edition of her book.
7. Let's ask how we should get to the train station.

UNIT 7 Lesson 2

Noun clauses with that: after mental activity verbs

The following verbs often have noun clauses as their direct objects. Notice that they are all a kind of mental activity. It is optional to include that.

agree	We agree (that) he should work harder.
assume	I assume (that) you made a reservation. Right?
believe	She believes (that) all people are created equal.
decide	We decided (that) we should stay another night.
discover	He discovered (that) the work hadn't been done yet.
doubt	I doubt (that) they really understand the problem.
dream	She dreamed (that) she was a movie star.
feel	We feel (that) everyone needs to try harder.
find out	I found out (that) the bill had already been paid.
forget	She forgot (that) she had been there once before.

guess	I guess (that) we'll just have to do it ourselves.	**notice**	Did you notice (that) they didn't call us back?
hear	He heard (that) they were planning another meeting.	**realize**	Do you realize (that) tomorrow is her birthday?
hope	I hope (that) everyone is OK.	**remember**	He remembered (that) he forgot to call home.
know	They know (that) we asked everyone to come at 8:00.	**see**	I see (that) you've finished everything.
learn	She learned (that) the book was written in 1933.	**suppose**	I suppose (that) you're hungry. Right?
		think	She thinks (that) everyone should help.
		understand	We understand (that) you're from Brazil. Is that right?

Noun clauses with that: after other expressions

Use noun clauses after these expressions with be + adjective or be + past participle.

be afraid that	I'm afraid (that) we'll have to leave early.
be angry that	She's angry (that) he never called.
be ashamed that	He's ashamed (that) he never called.
be disappointed that	We're disappointed (that) you couldn't come.
be happy that	They're happy (that) they passed the test.
be sad that	I'm sad (that) you're leaving.
be sorry that	We're sorry (that) we missed you.
be sure that	Are you sure (that) he's the man who did it?
be surprised that	She was surprised (that) she won.
be worried that	They're worried (that) he may be angry.

A On a separate sheet of paper, complete the sentences in your own way. Use noun clauses with that.

1. When I was young, I couldn't believe . . .
2. Last year, I decided . . .
3. Recently, I dreamed . . .
4. This year, I was surprised to discover . . .
5. Last week, I forgot . . .
6. Recently, I heard . . .
7. In the future, I hope . . .
8. Now that I study English, I know . . .
9. In the last year, I learned . . .
10. Not long ago, I remembered . . .
11. (Your own idea) . . .
12. (Your own idea) . . .

UNIT 8 Lesson 1

Unless in conditional sentences

You can use unless, instead of if not, in conditional sentences.

Unless they buy a freezer, they'll have to cook every night. = If they don't buy a freezer, …

She wouldn't drive a car **unless she had** a cell phone. = … if she didn't have a cell phone.

Martin doesn't buy electronics **unless they're** state of the art. = … if they're not state of the art.

On a separate sheet of paper, rewrite the sentences, changing if not statements to unless and making any necessary changes.

1. If you don't buy the Brew Rite coffee maker, you'll be sorry.
   Unless you buy the Brew Rite coffee maker, you'll be sorry.
2. If you aren't in a hurry, you should take the train.
3. If I didn't need to drive long distances, I wouldn't consider the top-of-the-line model.
4. She won't go running in the park if her friends don't go with her.
5. Claire won't buy a high-tech car if it doesn't have a good sound system.
6. I wouldn't get the one with cutting-edge technology if I weren't rich.

Clauses after wish

Use were or the simple past tense after wish to express a regret about something that's not true now.

I **wish** my laptop **were** top of the line.

We **wish** we **had** a Brew Rite coffee maker.

Use the past perfect after wish or wished to express a regret about something that was not true in the past.

Sean **wishes** he **hadn't sold** his car.

Sean **wished** he **hadn't sold** his car.

Use would and a base form after wish to express a desire that something will occur in the future or on a regular basis.

I wish it **would rain**. (present desire for a future occurrence)

I wish you **would help** with the housework more often. (desire for something to occur regularly)

Use would and a base form after wished to express a wish one had in the past for a future occurrence.

Yesterday I **wished** it **would rain**, but it didn't. (a wish for the future one had in the past)

B **Complete each statement or question with the correct form of the verb.**

1. I wish my favorite author _______________ (write) a new book. I've read all of his old books so many times.
2. Pat wished she _______________ (spend) more time test-driving cars before she bought that SUV.
3. Most people wish they _______________ (be) rich.
4. I wish it _______________ (be) possible for me to get a better camera last time.
5. They wished they _______________ (know) sooner that the computer couldn't be fixed.
6. When I was a child, my parents wished I _______________ (become) a doctor.
7. Do you wish you _______________ (have) a more comfortable car for the trip tomorrow?
8. Don't they wish they _______________ (study) German?
9. I wish I _______________ (be) married to a mechanic. My car keeps breaking down!

UNIT 8 Lesson 2

The unreal conditional: variety of forms

Unreal conditional sentences can have a variety of active and passive forms in either clause.

If he had worn a seat belt, he **wouldn't have been hurt**.

If the car **had been totaled**, she could have bought a new one.

If the computer hadn't been invented, we **would** still **be using** typewriters.

If the typewriter **were still being used**, fewer people would have computers.

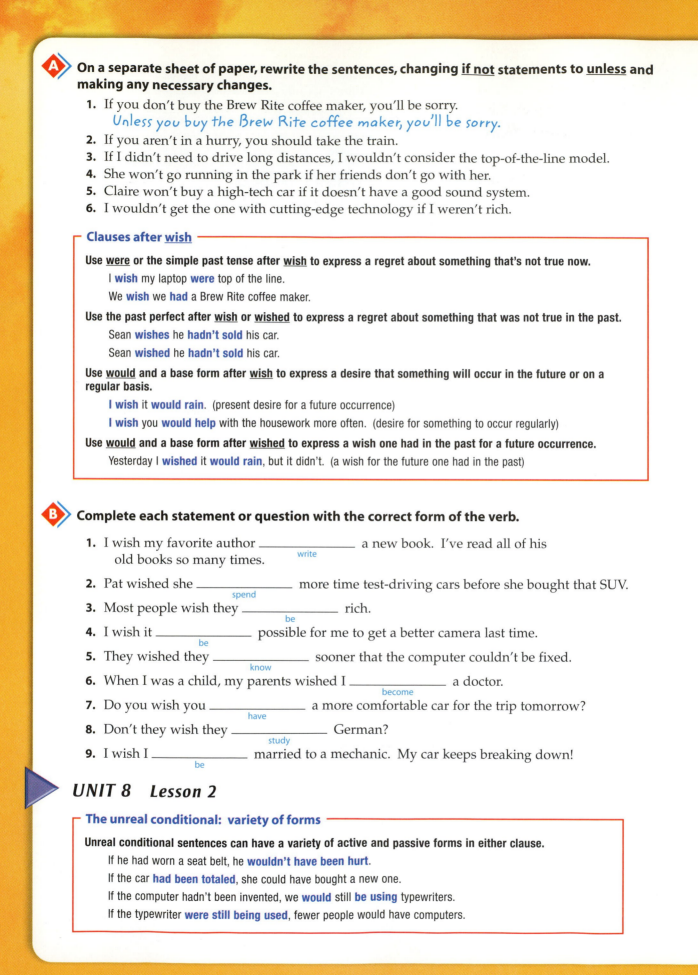

A Complete the following unreal conditional sentences in your own way, using active and passive forms.

1. If I were elected president, ______________________________.
2. The car would have been invented earlier if ______________________________.
3. If I were driving and another driver cut me off, ______________________________.
4. If they had been selling this phone when I was looking for one, ______________________________.
5. ______________________________, I wouldn't be studying English now.
6. If she were getting married today, ______________________________.

UNIT 9 Lesson 1

Count and non-count nouns

Count nouns name things that can be counted individually. They have singular and plural forms.

a president	presidents
a government	governments
a liberal	liberals
an election	elections
an official	officials

Non-count nouns name things that are not counted individually. They don't have singular or plural forms and they are not preceded by a or an. To express a specific quantity of an uncountable noun, use unit expressions.

a piece of news	a time of peace
a cup of tea	an act of justice
a kilo of rice	

Many nouns can be used as count or non-count nouns, but the meaning is different.

She studied **government** at the university. (= academic subject)
That country has had four **governments** in ten years. (= group of people who rule the country)

I love **cheese**. (in general)
I bought a **cheese**. (the whole manufactured product, such as a "wheel of cheese.")

She has blond **hair**. (in general = all of her hair)
She got a **hair** in her eye. (= one individual hair)

A Complete each sentence with the correct form of each noun.

1. The government has made ____________ (progress) in the economy.
2. They've given a lot of ____________ (importance) to making the banks stable.
3. Unfortunately, ____________ (radical) changed the law.
4. ____________ (peace) can only come if people stop making war.
5. ____________ (moderate) don't favor extreme change.
6. He's ____________ (reactionary) who would like to outlaw freedom of speech.
7. If I could give you one piece of ____________ (advice), it would be to vote.
8. Some ____________ (government) are more liberal than others.
9. If more people don't find ____________ (work), people will elect a different president.
10. It's impossible to end all ____________ (poverty).

UNIT 9 Lesson 2

Gerunds and infinitives: form

A gerund (the base form of a verb + -<u>ing</u>) functions as a noun. Gerunds can be subjects, objects, and subject complements.

Discussing politics is my favorite activity. (subject)

I love **reading** about government. (direct object)

I read a book about **voting**. (object of preposition <u>about</u>)

My favorite activity is **watching** TV news. (subject complement after <u>be</u>)

An infinitive (<u>to</u> + the base form of a verb) also functions as a noun.

To lie around on a beach all day would be my ideal vacation. (subject)

I love **to guess** who's going to win the election. (object)

My greatest dream for the summer is **to swim** every day. (subject complement after <u>be</u>)

A **Using the sentences in the box above as a model, write sentences on a separate sheet of paper using the gerunds and infinitives in the form shown.**

1. (as the subject of a sentence) Swimming
2. (as a direct object) driving
3. (as the object of the preposition <u>of</u>) studying
4. (as the subject of a sentence) To travel
5. (as a direct object) to eat

Review: Gerunds and infinitives after certain verbs

Certain verbs are followed by gerunds: <u>avoid</u>, <u>can't stand</u>, <u>discuss</u>, <u>dislike</u>, <u>enjoy</u>, <u>feel like</u>, <u>(don't) mind</u>, <u>practice</u>, <u>quit</u>, <u>suggest</u>.

Other verbs are followed by infinitives: <u>agree</u>, <u>choose</u>, <u>decide</u>, <u>expect</u>, <u>hope</u>, <u>learn</u>, <u>need</u>, <u>plan</u>, <u>seem</u>, <u>want</u>, <u>wish</u>, <u>would like</u>.

Other verbs can be followed by either a gerund or an infinitive: <u>begin</u>, <u>continue</u>, <u>hate</u>, <u>like</u>, <u>love</u>, <u>prefer</u>.

For a more complete list, see Appendix on page 130.

B **Complete the paragraph with gerunds or infinitives.**

I hope ______________ (make) some positive changes in my life, and I would like ______________ (start) right away. I have observed that a lot of people enjoy ______________ (complain) about the political situation, but they don't like ______________ (do) anything about it. They love ______________ (watch) the news and say they care about all the poor people who don't have enough to eat, but they don't feel like ______________ (do) anything about it. They worry about poverty but they don't mind ______________ (waste) money on stupid things they don't need ______________ (have). Well, I'm sick of ______________ (read) about how people are suffering, and I've agreed ______________ (join) a political action group. I simply hate ______________ (not do) anything!

UNIT 10 Lesson 1

A **Choose ten adjectives from the box. On a separate sheet of paper, write a sentence for each adjective. Use <u>too</u> and an infinitive to give an explanation or a warning.**

afraid	down in the dumps	high	sad
busy	early	important	sick
conservative	expensive	loud	self-critical
depressing	heavy	old	young

EXAMPLE: difficult *This homework is too difficult to finish in one hour.*

Infinitives with enough

Use an infinitive after an adjective or adverb and enough to give an explanation.

She's **old enough** to vote.
He's not **busy enough** to complain.
They drove **fast enough** to get there on time.
It isn't **warm enough to go** hiking today.

BE CAREFUL! Enough comes after an adjective or an adverb, not before.

It's **too far** to walk. It isn't **close enough** to walk. NOT ~~It isn't enough close to walk.~~

B On a separate sheet of paper, write a sentence with enough and an infinitive for each adjective in the box.

not old	smart	not strong	hungry
all	not calm	polite	thirsty
not responsible	not successful	not exciting	happy

UNIT 10 Lesson 2

Prepositions of place: more usage

It's **on**
- the Nicoya Peninsula.
- Easter Island.
- the Hudson River. (also: **along** the Hudson River.)
- Coronado Bay.
- the coast.
- Lake Placid.
- the Gulf of Aqaba.

It's **in**
- Cheju Province.
- the Rocky Mountains.
- the Central Valley.
- the Sahara Desert.
- the Atlantic Ocean.
- the state of Jalisco.

It's in the central part / It's southwest / It's about 50 km north } **of** Madrid.

A Write the correct prepositions of place.

1. Pisco is ____ the Pacific coast of Peru.
2. Tianjin, in China, is ____ Shendong Province.
3. Desaguadero is ____ Lake Titicaca in Bolivia.
4. The island of Bahrain is ____ the Persian Gulf.
5. Cabimas is ____ Lake Maracaibo in Venezuela.
6. Sapporo is ____ Hokkaido Island in Japan.
7. Riobamba is ____ the Pastaza River in Ecuador.
8. Taiwan's Jade Mountain National Park is east ____ the city of Alishan.
9. Fengkang is ____ the southern part ____ Taiwan.
10. The city of Budapest, Hungary is ____ the Danube River.
11. Denmark is north ____ Germany.
12. The capital of Chile, Santiago, is located ____ the Central Valley.

Proper nouns: capitalization

When words like east or southeast are used as the name of a place, they should be capitalized.

It's in **the South**. It's in **the Northeast**. It's in the **Middle East**.

When they are just used to describe a place, the words are not capitalized.

It's **south of** Taipei. It's a **northeastern** city. It's on the **eastern** shore of Lake Superior.

Capitalize names of:

people (and their titles)	Mary	Mary Smith	Dr. Mary Smith
places	Bolivia	the United Kingdom	Kyoto
buildings and public places	the Golden Gate Bridge	the Paramount Theater	the Tower of London
organizations	the U.N.	the World Bank	Amnesty International
religions	Christianity	Judaism	Islam
holidays	New Year's Day	the Moon Festival	Carnaval
historic times or events	the Cold War	the Middle Ages	the Edo Period
languages / nationalities	French	English	Arabic
the days of the week	Monday	Wednesday	Sunday
the months of the year	January	October	December

When a proper noun has more than one word, each word is capitalized except for articles (the) and prepositions (of).

Panama City | the Gulf of Aqaba | the City of Chicago
the University of Buenos Aires | Niagara Falls | the Bay of Biscayne

Capitalize all the words of a title, except for articles and prepositions that have fewer than four letters. If an article or a preposition is the first word of a title, capitalize it.

The Story of English | Looking Back on My Life
The International Herald Tribune | I Know Why the Caged Bird Sings

Correct the capitalization.

1. I'm reading one hundred years of solitude.
2. My cousins are studying french.
3. The leaning tower of pisa is in northern italy.
4. It's on the southern coast of australia.
5. I visit the city museum of art every monday.
6. My uncle works for the united nations.
7. The channel tunnel (chunnel) between england and france was completed in 1994.
8. She just graduated from the university of washington.
9. We enjoyed the movie about the great wall of china.
10. My son goes to the college of sciences.
11. His father speaks korean and japanese fluently.
12. Their grandson was born last march.

Proper nouns: use of the

When a proper noun includes the word of, use the.

with the	without the
the Republic of Korea	Korea
the Gulf of Mexico	Mexico City
the Kingdom of Thailand	Thailand

When a proper noun uses a political word such as republic, empire, or kingdom, use the.

the United Kingdom — the British Empire — the Malagasy Republic

When a proper noun is plural, use the.

the Philippines
the Netherlands
the United States
the Andes Mountains

When a proper noun includes a geographical word such as ocean, desert, or river, use the. Do not use the with the following geographical words: lake, bay, mountain, island, park.

with the	without the
the Atlantic Ocean	Hudson Bay
the Atacama Desert	Crystal Lake
the Yangze River	Hainan Island
the Iberian Peninsula	Ueno Park
the Persian Gulf	Yellow Mountain

When words like east or southwest are used as the name of a geographical area, use the. Do not use the when they are used as adjectives.

with the	without the
the Middle East	Western Europe
the Far East	East Timor
the West	Northern Ireland

When a proper noun includes a word that is a kind of organization or educational group, use the. Do not use the with a university or college (unless the name uses of).

with the	without the
the International Language Institute	Columbia College
the United Nations	Chubu University
the World Health Organization	
the University of Adelaide	

Do not use the with acronyms.

U.C.L.A. (the University of California, Los Angeles)
NATO (the North Atlantic Treaty Organization)
OPEC (the Organization of Petroleum Exporting Countries)

C Correct the sentences.

1. When she went to the Malaysia, she brought her husband with her.
2. A lot of people from United States teach English here.
3. The Haiti is the closest neighbor to Dominican Republic.
4. When we arrived in the Berlin, I was very excited.
5. Yemen is a country in Middle East.
6. I introduced our visitors to University of Riyadh.
7. I lived in People's Republic of China for about two years.
8. Yan is a student at College of Arts and Sciences.
9. She is the director of English Language Institute.
10. She's the most famous actress in Netherlands.
11. He's interested in cultures in Near East.
12. Poland was one of the first countries in the Eastern Europe to change to a democracy.

TOP NOTCH POP LYRICS

It's a Great Day for Love [Unit 1]

Wherever you go,
there are things you should know,
so be aware
of the customs and views—
all the do's and taboos—
of people there.
You were just a stranger in a sea of new faces.
Now we're making small talk on a first-name basis.
(CHORUS)
It's a great day for love, isn't it?
Aren't you the one I was hoping to find?
It's a great day for love, isn't it?
By the time you said hello,
I had already made up my mind.
Wherever you stay
be sure to obey
the golden rules,
and before you relax,
brush up on the facts
you learned at school.
Try to be polite and always be sure to get
some friendly advice on proper etiquette.
(CHORUS)
and when you smiled at me
and I fell in love,
the sun had just appeared
in the sky above.
You know how much I care, don't you?
And you'll always be there, won't you?
(CHORUS)

I'll Get Back to You [Unit 3]

Your camera isn't working right.
It needs a few repairs.
You make me ship it overnight.
Nothing else compares.
You had to lengthen your new skirt,
and now you want to get
someone to wash your fancy shirts
and dry them when they're wet.
Come a little closer—
let me whisper in your ear.
Is my message getting across
to you loud and clear?
(CHORUS)
You're always making plans.
I'll tell you what I'll do:
let me think it over and
I'll get back to you.
You want to get your suit dry-cleaned.
You want to get someone
to shorten your new pair of jeans
and call you when they're done.
I guess I'll have them print a sign
and hang it on your shelf,
with four small words in one big line:
"Just do it yourself."
Let me tell you what this song
is really all about.
I'm getting tired of waiting while you figure it out.
I've heard all your demands,
but I have a life too.
Let me think it over and
I'll get back to you.
I'm really reliable,
incredibly fast,
extremely helpful
from first to last.
Let me see what I can do.
Day after day,
everybody knows
I always do what I say.
(CHORUS)

Endless Holiday [Unit 5]

Day after day,
all my thoughts drift away
before they've begun.
I sit in my room
in the darkness and gloom
just waiting for someone
to take me to a tourist town,
with parties in the street and people
dancing to a joyful sound.
(CHORUS)
It's a song that people sing.
It's the laughter that you bring
on an endless holiday.
It's the happiness inside.
It's a roller coaster ride
on an endless holiday.
I try and I try
to work hard, but I
get lost in a daze,
and I think about
how sad life is without
a few good holidays.
I close my eyes, pull down the shade,
and in my imagination I am dancing in a big parade,
and the music is loud.
I get lost in the crowd
on an endless holiday.
It's a picnic at noon.
It's a trip to the moon
on an endless holiday,
with flags and confetti,
wild costumes and a great big marching band,
as we wish each other well
in a language we all understand.
The sky above fills with the light
of fireworks exploding, as we dance along
the street tonight.
(CHORUS)

Lucky to Be Alive [Unit 6]

(CHORUS)
Thank you for helping me to survive.
I'm really lucky to be alive.
When I was caught in a freezing snowstorm,
you taught me how to stay warm.
When I was running from a landslide
with no place to hide,
you protected me from injury.
Even the world's biggest tsunami
has got nothing on me,
because you can go faster.
You keep me safe from disaster.
You're like some kind of hero—
you're the best friend that I know.
(CHORUS)
When the big flood came with
the pouring rain,
they were saying that a natural
disaster loomed.
You just opened your umbrella.
You were the only fellow who kept calm
and prepared.
You found us shelter.
I never felt like anybody cared
the way that you did when you said,
"I will always be there—
you can bet your life on it."
And when the cyclone turned the day into night,
you held a flashlight and showed me the
safe way home.
You called for help on your cell phone.
You said you'd never leave me.
You said, "Believe me,
in times of trouble you will never be alone."
They said it wasn't such a bad situation.
It was beyond imagination.
I'm just glad to be alive—
and that is no exaggeration.
(CHORUS)

Reinvent the Wheel [Unit 8]

You've got your digi camera with the Powershot,
four mega pixels and a memory slot.
You've got your e-mail and your Internet.
You send me pictures of your digi pet.
I got the digi dog and the digi cat,
the digi this and the digi that.
I hate to be the one to break the news,
but you're giving me the digi blues.
(CHORUS)
And you don't know
the way I really feel.
Why'd you have to go and
reinvent the wheel?
You've got your cordless phone and your microwave,
and your Reflex Plus for the perfect shave.
It's super special, top of the line,
with the latest new, cutting-edge design.
You've got your SLR and your LCD,
your PS2 and your USB.
I've seen the future and it's pretty grim:
they've used up all the acronyms.
(CHORUS)
I keep waiting for a breakthrough innovation:
something to help our poor communication.
Hey, where'd you get all of that high-tech taste?
Your faith in progress is such a waste.
Your life may be state of the art,
but you don't understand the human heart.
(CHORUS)